MW01041360

Figure.1
Vancouver / Berkeley

UBC
The Next Century

TYEE BRIDGE
FOREWORD BY SANTA J. ONO

Contents

Foreword

"Inspiring people, ideas and actions for a better world."

THAT'S THE VISION of the University of British Columbia. It's a vision of education as a catalyst, and it's entwined with the university's purpose, as laid out in our strategic plan: "Pursuing excellence in research, learning and engagement to foster global citizenship and advance a sustainable and just society across British Columbia, Canada and the world."

That's a big goal, and it's also the right one. Universities need to inspire their students to great achievements and encourage them to look beyond their horizons. The book that you're holding shows how UBC and its people—students, faculty, staff and graduates—are implementing that vision and achieving that purpose.

This book is not intended to be a history of UBC—that fascinating story has already been told in Sheldon Goldfarb's *The Hundred-Year Trek* and Eric Damer and Herbert Rosengarten's monumental *UBC: The First 100 Years*. While there are some important acknowledgements of our history, this book focuses on revealing UBC as it is today and the pathways we are making into the future.

One hundred years after it was founded, UBC stands as one of the world's foremost universities. Very few institutions can claim to have

above Professor
Santa J. Ono, UBC
President and
Vice-Chancellor.

joined the ranks of the world's top academic institutions in just one century, but UBC has achieved that milestone.

UBC's graduates excel in practically every field of human endeavour. Three graduates have served as prime minister of Canada, 70 graduates have been awarded the Rhodes Scholarship and 65 graduates have won Olympic medals.

The university now spans two magnificent campuses in Vancouver and the Okanagan, encompassing more than 1,500 acres. These campuses house some of the most advanced facilities for modern research in the world, including the Stewart Blusson Quantum Matter Institute and TRIUMF, Canada's national laboratory for particle and nuclear physics.

Along with downtown Vancouver locations at Robson Square and the Learning Exchange, UBC's presence includes a partnership in the Great Northern Way campus of the Centre for Digital Media; 11 clinical academic campuses; a dairy education and research centre in Agassiz; and research forests in Maple Ridge and Williams Lake.

UBC is also home to cutting-edge laboratories in the basic, applied and biomedical sciences. Site-directed mutagenesis (the ability to alter genes, a pillar of biotechnology) was invented here, and UBC is at the frontier of research on cancer genomics and personalized medicine. We rank within the top 30 globally—and, in many cases, much higher—in disciplines such as psychology, education, law, business and economics, life sciences, social sciences and computer science.

The university is, in short, a research powerhouse. This strength enriches our teaching: students at UBC learn from the best in the world. Eight UBC-associated individuals have been awarded the Nobel Prize, and our researchers have won numerous other national and international awards.

Complementing this environment of academic achievement is a culture of adventure, celebration and personal growth. Our students—who come here from every part of British Columbia, across Canada and around the world—are bright, passionate and committed to building a better future. They also know how to have fun. UBC's sports and recreation programs are legendary, and student events like Day of the LongBoat and the Block Party live on as enduring memories for all who participate.

I am proud of the University of British Columbia as it heads into its next century, and I am excited to be a part of it. Great things lie behind us, and great things are ahead.

Professor Santa J. Ono
President and Vice-Chancellor,
The University of British Columbia

above In every season, UBC's Point Grey campus reflects the beauty of its coastal surroundings.

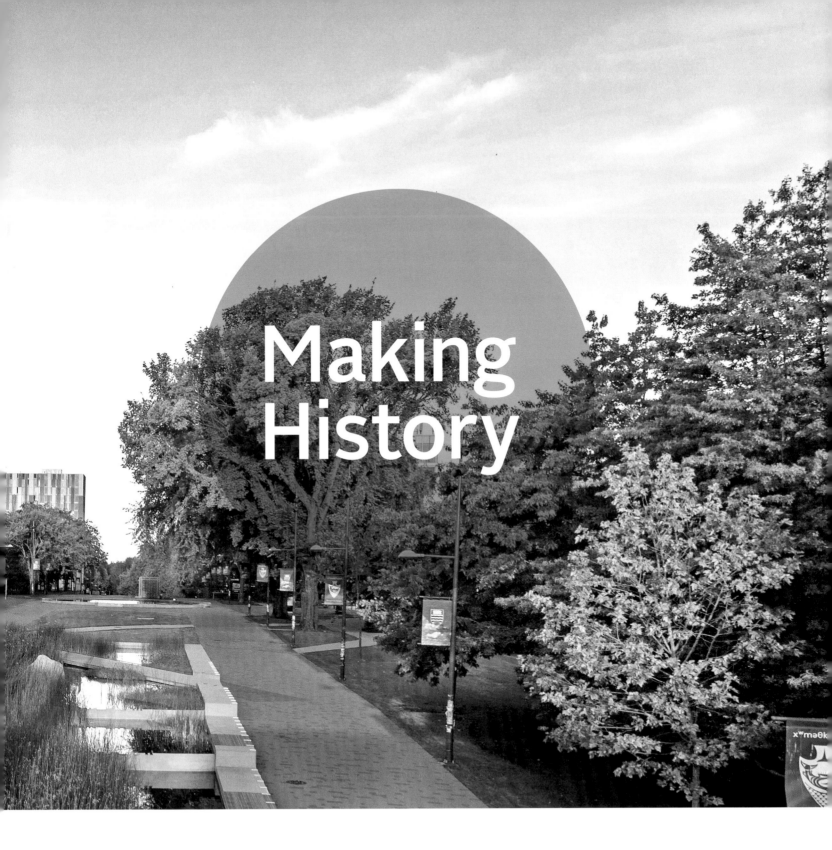

Making History

above Musqueam community members gathered for the raising of *Double-Headed Serpent Post*, also known as *Musqueam Post*, in 2016.

UBC and the Musqueam People

UBC's Point Grey campus is located on the traditional, unceded and ancestral territory of the Musqueam people. The Musqueam have lived in this area for thousands of years. Traditionally they caught salmon, eulachon and other fish, hunted and trapped game, and gathered food and medicines from the forests and beaches across what is now called the Lower Mainland.

"Our people have lived on this delta since the last ice age, approximately 10,000 years ago, always living at the mouth of the river," said Larry Grant, Elder-in-Residence at UBC's First Nations House of Learning. "As the delta was formed, we moved down and moved down, and we have lived continuously in our community of Musqueam for 4,000 years or more."

The Musqueam define their community's traditional territorial lands as including the watershed east of Lions Bay that drains into Burrard Inlet and Indian Arm, and the Lower Fraser west of the site of the Port Mann Bridge extending all the way to Ladner. Due to expropriation by successive waves of settlers, however, their reserve near UBC is now only 470 acres—an area that is, in the words of Musqueam curator and writer Jordan Wilson, "postage-stamp small." The Musqueam describe themselves currently as a "thriving community" that numbers over 1,400 people, nearly half of whom live in xʷməθkʷəy̓əm (Musqueam) village only a few kilometres from UBC.

In 2006 the Musqueam and UBC signed a memorandum of affiliation, which emphasized that both "understand the importance of building a long-term relationship." A number of initiatives have resulted, such as the Bridge Through Sport program, the Musqueam 101 speaker series and hən̓q̓əmin̓əm̓ (Musqueam) language classes.

During UBC's centennial year celebrations in 2015–2016, Musqueam artist Brent Sparrow Jr. carved the sʔi:ɫqəy̓ qeqən (*Double-Headed Serpent Post*) to celebrate the origin story of his people and acknowledge their developing relationship with UBC. Also known as *Musqueam Post*, the 10-metre pole faces east toward the new Robert H. Lee Alumni Centre and the campus entrance, and offers an enduring welcome to visitors.

Regarding the dedication of the post, Musqueam Chief Wayne Sparrow said, "We cherish the relationship between the university and the Musqueam. As UBC is on our traditional territory, it's important that we work together closely to share our culture and look for opportunities to work together."

above Chief Wayne Sparrow of the Musqueam.

MAKING HISTORY

above sʔi:ɬqəy̓ qeqən (*Double-Headed Serpent Post*) on UBC's Point Grey campus, carved by Brent Sparrow Jr. of the Musqueam.

The Musqueam continue to collaborate with the university in raising awareness of a post-colonial history of exclusion and marginalization—while co-creating educational programs and partnerships to benefit Indigenous peoples and all Canadians.

A Difficult Beginning

The University of British Columbia almost never happened. While there were proposals for a university as early as the 1870s—when the entire population of the province, at around 50,000 people, was less than UBC's current enrolment—it wasn't until 1908 that the legislature passed a bill called *An Act to Establish and Incorporate a University for the Province of British Columbia.*

One of the primary forces behind the act was Henry Esson Young, a Quebec-born doctor who had been elected a BC MLA in 1903 and was later appointed minister of education and provincial secretary. Legislation alone, however, does not a university make. It took a lot of planning, money and handshakes—and a good bit of student activism—to get UBC off the page and into history.

In 1913 the provincial government appointed Frank F. Wesbrook as the university's first president, and agreed to set aside $1.5 million to clear land and start building the Point Grey campus. Born in Ontario, Wesbrook was also a doctor like Young and had served as the dean of medicine at the University of Minnesota before being selected for the UBC presidency.

Wesbrook envisioned UBC as "a Provincial University without provincialism. May our sympathies be so broadened and our service so extended to all the people of the Province that we may indeed be the people's University, whose motto is *Tuum Est*."

Substantive progress was just starting to be made, including the steel-and-concrete construction of the Science Building, when World War I broke out in 1914. Construction was put on hold to marshal resources for the war effort, and the three-storey skeleton of the Science Building looked like it was going to be a headstone marking British Columbia's hopes for a provincial university.

But in spite of the war, things did move ahead—slowly. In 1915 classes were opened in "shacks" in Fairview near Vancouver General Hospital, offering a limited number of classes to a student body of

left Students on the Great Trek form the letters *UBC* on their yet-to-be-developed campus.

right Great Trek students pose on the exposed floors and roof of the Science Building.

379 people. Humble conditions didn't deter young people from applying; student enrolment tripled by 1922.

By then, conditions at Fairview were overcrowded and students were getting restless. In 1922 the student Alma Mater Society (AMS) began a "Build the University" campaign and collected 56,000 signatures for a petition. On October 28, UBC students participated in the famous protest pilgrimage later called the Great Trek—all 1,178 of them marching with banners, floats and musical instruments from downtown Vancouver to Point Grey.

Once on the grounds of their long-delayed campus, they assembled themselves for two well-considered and widely publicized photo ops. One shows them all sitting on the bare floors and roof of the Science Building's concrete frame; in another they've arranged themselves on the ground into a massive *UBC*. Student leaders Ab Richards, Jack Grant and J.V. Clyne followed up their media-savvy Trek with a trip to Victoria to present their petition to cabinet.

It worked. Premier John Oliver had been dubious about the merits of spending public money on building the university, but he and his officials relented and agreed to fund the needed work. The Science Building was completed in 1923, and a library in 1925. Construction began in 1924 on six new buildings that included administrative space, an auditorium and classroom spaces for agriculture, arts and applied sciences.

On September 22, 1925, about 1,400 students attended their first day of classes at their newly built university.

above Frank F. Wesbrook, UBC's first president, 1913–1918.

UBC Presidents

Santa J. Ono 15th president 2016–	**David W. Strangway** 10th president 1985–1997	**F. Kenneth Hare** 5th president 1968–1969
Martha C. Piper 14th president 2015–2016	**Robert H.T. Smith** 9th president 1985	**John B. Macdonald** 4th president 1962–1967
Arvind Gupta 13th president 2014–2015	**K. George Pedersen** 8th president 1983–1985	**Norman A.M. MacKenzie** 3rd president 1944–1962
Stephen J. Toope 12th president 2006–2014	**Douglas T. Kenny** 7th president 1975–1983	**Leonard S. Klinck** 2nd president 1919–1944
Martha C. Piper 11th president 1997–2006	**Walter H. Gage** 6th president 1969–1975	**Frank F. Wesbrook** 1st president 1913–1918

above Musqueam banner on University Boulevard.

President Wesbrook's Latin motto *Tuum Est* has usually been translated as "It Is Yours," and though he would never see his plans for a university realized—having passed away near the end of the war in 1918—UBC students took his vision and marched it into existence.

Acknowledging Traditional Territory

At the opening of university gatherings and events, students and other participants often hear an acknowledgement of the Indigenous territory on which they live, work and play.

These statements and their variations in other locations—other UBC programs in Metro Vancouver, for example, lie within territory shared by the Musqueam, Squamish and Tsleil-Waututh peoples—are a small gesture that recognizes the status of Indigenous peoples in British Columbia.

They acknowledge a history marred by injustice, racism and exclusion, and convey an intention to build a better relationship. Remembrances like these attempt to restore a better understanding of where we are, and with whom we live.

"Here at UBC on the Vancouver campus, when we make this acknowledgement, we're acknowledging history but also our present relationship with Musqueam and with other Indigenous communities

above Mary L. Bollert,
UBC's first dean of women.

in Canada and worldwide," explained Linc Kesler, a professor with the First Nations and Indigenous Studies program and former director of the First Nations House of Learning.

"The university is committed to access to education for Indigenous people, and to collaborative research relationships that work to the benefit of Indigenous communities, rather than to their detriment. And beyond that, to curriculum that will help students better understand the issues that are of importance to Indigenous communities, and their history. These are the foundations of potential future relationships."

Women and Equality at UBC

When provincial legislators passed the *British Columbia University Act* in 1908, they declared that the newly founded University of British Columbia would be not just non-sectarian but "co-educational"—that is, open to women as well as men. Administrators were true to their word, but in practice this egalitarian promise fell somewhat short. In *UBC: The First 100 Years,* historians described the situation in the 1920s this way: "As before, many academic courses were 'gendered,' with women discouraged from entering the sciences and agriculture (although many did well in the life sciences) and informally barred from engineering."

left 2013 spring graduation.

right Students in the Irving K. Barber Learning Centre.

Another history of UBC (*It's Up to You*, by Lee Stewart) argued that "boys' rules" differed substantially from "girls' rules" at UBC for many years, and that the literal translation of UBC's motto—*Tuum Est* in Latin, often rendered as "It Is Yours"—applied far more to men than it did to women.

In response, UBC's female students and graduates fought for true equality and recognition for decades. The University Women's Club and the BC Women's Network successfully campaigned for a dean of women in 1921. The university's first women's residence opened in 1951, and 20 years later UBC became the first Canadian university to offer a women's studies program. Women's studies has been offered as an undergraduate major at UBC since 1991.

Enrolment of female students at UBC has grown. Women now make up 60 per cent of the student body. The AMS Women's Centre reaches out to female students with resources, a safe space and empowering events, while two academic groups—the Women in Engineering group and the Women in Science Club—continue to overcome historical exclusion by supporting women's success in traditionally male-dominated sciences.

Ladner Clock Tower

UBC's clock tower stands over 37 metres high and is officially named the Ladner Carillon and Clock Tower—though it is most often referred to simply as the Ladner Clock Tower.

Completed in 1968, the tower displays four two-metre clock faces and houses a 330-bell carillon. The coloured lights along its top and sides were designed to be seen from all over campus, as well as from the waters off Point Grey.

Controversy arose during construction, when many students raised their eyebrows at the tower and its associated cost of $150,000. Campus newspaper *The Ubyssey* reported in 1967 that some student senators were requesting the funds be "diverted into more urgent projects, such as the library." Another student, reflecting the anti-authoritarian sentiments of the day, dismissed the clock tower and its tolling bells as "a large Pavlovian-type experiment."

above The Ladner Clock Tower, a UBC landmark since 1968.

MAKING HISTORY

above Restored in 2018, the Ladner Clock Tower once again chimes for UBC students and visitors.

After the tower was built, UBC administrators were hesitant to organize an opening ceremony for fear of giving students a venue for a protest. Instead, it was officially presented to the university at a quiet dinner party.

Over the years, student ire about the clock died down, and the tower has become an iconic landmark for the campus. On two occasions (once in the 1980s, and once in 2014) the shell of a Volkswagen Beetle was found on top of the tower—part of an ongoing tradition of such pranks perpetrated by undergraduate engineering students.

When President Santa Ono was inducted in 2016, the clock was in disrepair, with neither the clock nor tower lights in working order. To honour its 50th anniversary and the "unsung heroes" of the UBC Thunderbirds sports and recreation programs, President Ono had the clock restored in 2018. Today, the clock once again chimes out the hours and the lights glow steadily in the university's signature colours of blue and gold.

UBC Okanagan and the Syilx Okanagan Nation

Unlike the Vancouver campus, UBC Okanagan wasn't built from the ground up. Formerly known as Okanagan University College (OUC), for years it had consisted of a gymnasium, a courtyard and four brick buildings for classes and administration—along with two residence halls and a daycare.

OUC opened in 1993 on the sloping lands of a former quarry. After 10 years of operation, the provincial government announced that it would boost post-secondary education in the BC Interior by bringing the college under the auspices of UBC.

UBC Okanagan officially opened in 2005 with an enrolment of 3,500 students and Barry McBride as inaugural deputy vice-chancellor. The new institution was welcomed to the region by the Syilx Okanagan Nation in an official ceremony.

above Between classes at the UBC Okanagan campus.

Elder Victor
Antoine of the Okana-
gan Indian Band
offered the opening
prayer at the 2005
ceremony in which
the Okanagan Nation
Alliance welcomed
UBC to the territory
of the Syilx Okanagan
people.

Syilx Okanagan territory encompasses an area of about 69,000 square kilometres, with the northern portion extending past Revel-stoke and the southern reaching into Washington State. Historically, a Syilx Okanagan village was located near what is now the UBC Okanagan campus, and the surrounding area was used for harvesting game, berries and other traditional foods.

At the 2005 ceremony, the university and the Syilx Okanagan Nation signed a memorandum of understanding committing them to educational cooperation, and on UBC Okanagan's 10th anniversary, both parties formally re-signed the agreement.

"We have come a long way together, and we have a very strong working relationship with this campus," said Westbank First Nation Chief Robert Louie at the anniversary. "We work together in cooper-ation and friendship to promote academic excellence for all of our students. It makes us proud to see the achievements and to know that the Okanagan Syilx people are part of that."

Since 2005, UBC Okanagan has tripled the floor space of its facilities with new infrastructure—such as the 70,000-square-foot Charles E. Fipke Centre for Innovative Research—and seen enrol-ment grow to over 9,000 students.

above Officially opened in 2005, UBC Okanagan now enrolls 9,000 students annually.

left The Okanagan Nation Alliance flag in the main courtyard of UBC Okanagan was first raised in a 2018 ceremony by UBC students from the Okanagan Indian Band and the Westbank First Nation.

facing Named for
one of UBC's most
dedicated graduates,
the Robert H.
Lee Alumni Centre
opened in 2015.

Alumni UBC

In 1916 there were only 40 students in UBC's first graduating class. Due to World War I, construction of the campus at Point Grey in Vancouver had ground to a halt, and it wasn't certain that it would ever be built—or that the university itself would even continue. Vancouver's modest new grove of academe needed help if it was ever going to thrive.

Enter the UBC Alumni Association, formed in 1917 by some of the university's earliest graduates. For over a hundred years the association has worked to improve the fortunes of UBC and its alumni through events, fundraising and publications.

Fundraising was shifted to the university's development office in 1989, and now alumni UBC serves over 337,000 alumni in 148 countries with a variety of programs and benefits. *Trek* magazine features stories about graduates and other university news in two print and two online-only issues each year.

Leadership committees in five alumni-rich regions—Victoria, Toronto, Calgary, Hong Kong and the Okanagan—support professional development and keep alumni connected to each other and to the university itself.

Perhaps the biggest evolutionary leap for alumni UBC in recent years was the opening of the $18.5-million Robert H. Lee Alumni Centre, which offers a striking new space dedicated to alumni resources and events.

Robert H. Lee Alumni Centre

Completed in 2015, the Robert H. Lee Alumni Centre sits at the heart of the UBC campus. Visitors are welcomed into a light-filled, West Coast–inspired space—lots of glass and locally milled BC wood—that includes a café, a fireplace lounge, study spaces and an open library. An angular wood staircase zigzags through the atrium, inspired by a two-headed serpent that is central to the origin story of the Musqueam people.

On the upper floors, visitors to the 4,700-square-foot Jack Poole Hall get spectacular views of campus through the 14-foot windows. It's a sought-after setting for galas, conferences, weddings, corporate retreats and private events.

The centre was designed by KPMB Architects and named for one of UBC's most dedicated alumni. A graduate of UBC's class of 1956, Robert H. "Bob" Lee met his wife, Lily (also class of 1956), at UBC, and their four children also went on to graduate from their parents' alma mater.

Lee founded the property development and management firm Prospero Group, and has assisted UBC in various capacities for over 30 years—he joined the board of governors in 1984 and has served as chancellor and as chair of the UBC Foundation.

Lee's contributions helped create the Robert H. Lee Graduate School at the Sauder School of Business, and he founded the UBC Properties Trust in 1988, which has generated tremendous returns for the university's endowment fund.

UBC Properties Trust

As part of the ever present discussion of how to raise funds for the university's endowment, Robert H. Lee had an idea: build for-sale market housing on some of the university's lands. The developments would be given a 99-year lease so that the land would ultimately remain in UBC's possession.

Despite some initial reservations on the part of then president David Strangway and some of Lee's fellow board members, Lee convinced them to give his idea a try. The board of governors tested his idea "conservatively" at first, Lee said, perhaps not aware at the time that—with Vancouver poised to become one of the hottest real estate markets on the planet—they were sitting on a gold mine. By 1998, the plan, known as the UBC Properties Trust, had netted UBC $81 million through the building of its first neighbourhood, Hampton Place.

To say Lee's plan worked would be understating it. It has not been without controversy in all cases, but since the inception of the Properties Trust, UBC has developed 200 acres of land into neighbourhood communities that now house over 12,000 people. Along the way, the university raised an incredible amount of money for its endowment fund: $1.6 billion at last count, with another $2.5 billion expected to come over the next two decades.

The university's move into real estate "will probably make UBC's endowment one of the largest in the world," said Lee at a 2019 celebration marking his retirement from the Properties Trust. "It will certainly over time help move UBC into the front ranks of the world's foremost research institutions. It is an investment in the future of UBC and generations of students to come."

facing The wood-panelled staircase inside the Robert H. Lee Alumni Centre.

top Justin Trudeau, appointed prime minister in 2015, addressing a crowd at UBC Okanagan.

bottom Kim Campbell, appointed prime minister in 1993.

ALUMNI: Prime Ministers

Three UBC graduates have risen to be prime minister of Canada—leading the country from the relatively chilly and decidedly distant capital of Ottawa.

Justin Trudeau

Justin Trudeau graduated from UBC with a Bachelor of Education in 1998, teaching French and math in Vancouver before becoming involved in politics in the early 2000s. After becoming the leader of the Liberal Party in 2013, he won the general election of 2015 and was appointed prime minister.

Kim Campbell

Kim Campbell, Canada's first female prime minister, earned her Bachelor of Arts in Political Science at UBC, graduating in 1969. She studied at the London School of Economics before returning to UBC for her law degree, which was awarded in 1983. Her political career began in provincial politics soon after she graduated, and she moved into the federal arena as a member of the Progressive Conservative Party, serving both as justice minister and minister of national defence before following Brian Mulroney as leader of the party and prime minister in 1993.

John Turner

John Turner studied political science at UBC, graduating in 1949, and went on to study law at Oxford. His political career with the Liberal Party began in 1957; it spanned many years and many appointments, including minister of justice and minister of finance. He became prime minister after winning the Liberal leadership when Prime Minister Pierre Trudeau retired in 1984.

above John Turner, appointed prime minister in 1984.

ALUMNI: Leaders in the Law

UBC students study how to practise law at the Peter A. Allard School of Law, which has an international reputation for shaping outstanding legal minds.

Graduates of the law school at UBC have left their mark on Canadian jurisprudence by serving on the Supreme Court of Canada, the British Columbia Court of Appeal, the Supreme Court of British Columbia and the Provincial Court of British Columbia.

Judge of the Supreme Court of Canada
Frank Iacobucci

The child of Italian immigrants, Justice Iacobucci grew up in East Vancouver and paid for his UBC law degree by working at a steel foundry. A member of the class of 1962, after earning his Bachelor of Laws he held a private practice in New York before serving as dean of the Faculty of Law at the University of Toronto.

Justice Iacobucci served as Canada's deputy minister of justice and deputy attorney general before being appointed chief justice of the Federal Court of Canada in 1988. In 1989 UBC recognized his achievements with an honorary Doctor of Laws degree. From 1991 to 2004 he served as a judge of the Supreme Court of Canada. He worked on a variety of provincial and federal issues, including acting as the federal negotiator for the Indian residential schools settlement.

Chief Justices of the British Columbia Court of Appeal
Lance Sidney George Finch

Justice Finch earned his Bachelor of Laws at UBC in 1962. He held a private practice for two decades before being appointed to the Supreme Court of British Columbia in 1983—only a year after the Charter of Rights and Freedoms came into law.

He was appointed to the British Columbia and Yukon courts of appeal in 1993, and in 2001 he was appointed chief justice of both courts. In 2003 Justice Finch received an honorary Doctor of Laws degree from UBC. He retired from the courts of appeal in 2013, and that same year the law school's alumni association presented him with the Lifetime Achievement Award. In 2017 he was named to the Order of British Columbia in recognition of his legal decisions in cases relating to Indigenous rights and title, and for his status as "a role model for how to be and do the difficult business of judging."

Allan McEachern

Justice McEachern earned his law degree from UBC in 1950. After 28 years of private practice, he was appointed chief justice of the Supreme Court of British Columbia in 1979, and he went on to serve as chief justice of the British Columbia Court of Appeal from 1988 to 2001.

UBC awarded Justice McEachern an honorary Doctor of Laws degree in 1990. During his career he held a variety of other notable positions, including director of the Vancouver Bar Association, president of the Legal Aid Society, president of the BC Lions and president and commissioner of the Canadian Football League.

Alumni

Chief Justices of the Supreme Court of British Columbia:
Christopher E. Hinkson, 2013–present (LLB 1975)
Donald I. Brenner, 2000–2009 (LLB 1970)
Bryan Williams, 1996–2000 (LLB 1958)
William A. Esson, 1989–1996 (LLB 1957)
Allan McEachern, 1979–1988 (LLB 1950, LLD 1990)

Chief Judges of the Provincial Court of British Columbia:
Hugh C. Stansfield, 2005–2009 (LLB 1979)
Carol Baird Ellan, 2000–2005 (LLB 1979)
Robert W. Metzger, 1995–2000 (LLB 1973)
William J. Diebolt, 1989–1995 (LLB 1971)
Gerald R.B. Coultas, 1983–1988 (LLB 1955)
Lawrence S. Goulet, 1978–1983 (LLB 1961)
Lawrence C. Brahan, 1972–1978 (LLB 1959)
Cyril White, 1970–1972 (LLB 1949)

above and facing
UBC students are on
the leading edge of
research, technology
and sustainability.

Shaping UBC's Next Century

In 2018 UBC launched a new strategic plan, *Shaping UBC's Next Century.* Focusing on core themes of inclusion, collaboration and innovation, the plan builds on the ethos and achievements of the previous strategic plan, *Place and Promise.*

Intended as a roadmap to guide the decisions of university leaders, as well as the allocation of funding and other resources, the new plan defines UBC's ambitions through 20 strategies. Along with striving for environmental sustainability and student wellness, these include testing innovative and experiential teaching methods; developing interdisciplinary research clusters to tackle social challenges; and engaging with Indigenous communities in the long work of reconciliation.

"We want to inspire the very best in our students, faculty, staff, alumni and partners, and we recognize the degree to which we continue to be inspired by the people and the communities with whom we work," wrote President and Vice-Chancellor Santa Ono on the eve of the launch.

"This is our moment to harness the energies and strengths of an extraordinary institution to contribute to sustainable and positive change, both locally and globally."

Excellence in Teaching and Learning

above The 155,000-square-foot Djavad Mowafaghian Centre for Brain Health opened on UBC's Point Grey campus in 2014.

Faculty of Medicine

The UBC Faculty of Medicine is known for innovations in research and education that are propelling students toward new futures in healthcare.

That tradition continues to move ahead at full steam. In addition to major funding for new genetics research (see page 119), several new initiatives are helping keep the faculty's graduates on the leading edge of healthcare education and delivery.

One of the more striking is the department's collaboration with Vancouver-based Microsoft Garage on the creation of an interactive teaching tool called the HoloLens, which uses "mixed reality" to help students explore the makeup of the human brain.

"The human brain is extremely complicated, and that makes neuroanatomy difficult to learn and teach," said Dr. Claudia Krebs, a professor of anatomy who is helping lead the project. "We're very excited to be introducing the world of mixed reality into the classroom."

UBC graduate Edwin S.H. Leong kick-started another emergent program at the Faculty of Medicine in 2018 by donating toward the development of the Edwin S.H. Leong Healthy Aging Program. Along with improving outcomes in quality of life, the program's focus is a better understanding—based on personal biology and history—of individual predispositions toward disease. The centre is attracting leading researchers from across disciplines toward finding and promoting new paths to increased longevity.

Following the 15th anniversary of the Indigenous MD Admissions program—which has seen more than 80 Indigenous students become doctors in British Columbia and across Canada—in 2018 the Faculty of Medicine launched Canada's first certificate program in Indigenous public health. Training in health policy, biostatistics and environmental health will give participants the skills needed to address health inequities and public health issues in Indigenous communities across the country and beyond.

above Dr. Rebekah Eatmon, a graduate of UBC's medical program, is among the more than 90 Indigenous medical alumni now working in diverse communities throughout BC and Canada.

above Dr. Nadine Caron, 1997 graduate of the Faculty of Medicine and Canada's first female Indigenous surgeon.

ALUMNI
Dr. Nadine Caron

When Dr. Nadine Caron graduated from UBC's Faculty of Medicine in 1997, she accomplished two firsts: she was not only first in her class, but also the first Indigenous woman in history to graduate from the university's medical school.

This has been a trend for Caron. After earning her Master of Public Health from Harvard University, she returned to British Columbia as the first female Indigenous surgeon in Canada. A role model for medical students and Indigenous youth hoping to blaze their own trails of service and excellence, Caron currently works as a general and endocrine surgeon in Prince George and in UBC's Northern Medical Program as an assistant professor.

Caron also spearheads a groundbreaking new initiative called the Northern Biobank. The project—the first of its kind in North America—stores and documents tissue samples from Northern populations for personalized medical research.

Asian Studies

What makes a university Asian studies program great? Situated on the Pacific Rim, UBC has a geographical advantage over many institutions, but as with so many things, it's content that counts—and a long history doesn't hurt either.

The Department of Asian Studies launched in 1961. The department now offers more than 80 courses in Asian history, literature, film, popular culture, linguistics and gender, among many other subject areas—even some examining the narratives of manga comics and anime.

With nearly 60 full-time faculty members, the department sums up its mission this way: "Above all, we aim for our students to leave our program with the confidence to contribute to North America's evolving relationship with Asia in informed, original and culturally appropriate ways."

To this end, students can receive instruction in nine Asian languages: Cantonese, Chinese, Hindi-Urdu, Japanese, Korean, Persian, Punjabi, Sanskrit and Tibetan. The new comprehensive Cantonese language program is currently the only for-credit university-level course of its kind in Canada.

above The UBC Asian Studies Department oversees the Asian Centre, which houses a library, conference spaces and a gallery suitable for tea ceremonies.

above Students at a festive gathering at the Asian Centre.

In 2011 the UBC senate approved measures to acknowledge and remember the 76 Japanese Canadian students who in 1942, following the outbreak of war with Japan, were removed from UBC and sent to internment camps, along with 21,000 other Japanese Canadians. One of these measures was the creation of the Asian Canadian and Asian Migration (ACAM) Studies minor program, which explores Asian migrations and the history and development of Asian communities in Canada.

The Asian Studies Department collaborates on the ACAM minor with several other departments—including Geography, History, English Language and Literatures, and First Nations and Indigenous Studies—to offer students another unique program that will deepen their understanding of Canada's relationship with Asia.

Engineering

Part of the Faculty of Applied Science, Engineering has been a foundational and highly regarded program at UBC since it was founded in 1915. The program continues to stay on the leading edge of new technologies and approaches, particularly through new interdisciplinary departments and initiatives.

The School of Biomedical Engineering is a collaboration between the Faculty of Medicine and the Faculty of Applied Science. It welcomed its first cohort of undergraduates in 2018, giving students a head start on the skills that will enable them to succeed in a rapidly developing field. Work in this area is gaining wider recognition as researchers continue to invent and refine life-saving healthcare interventions such as new pharmaceuticals, dialysis technologies, advanced prosthetics, artificial organs and even robots with surgical capabilities.

In 2011 a new facility boosted student resources for interdisciplinary teamwork: the Wayne and William White Engineering Design Centre connects students from across the Faculty of Applied Science and gives them space for hands-on engineering and collaborative project-based learning. The three-storey centre encompasses 20,000 square feet and includes classrooms and meeting rooms, study spaces and specialized workspaces. One workshop provides students with 3-D printers, workbenches, power tools and prototyping machinery.

above A civil engineering postdoctoral researcher tests a new composite road material made with recycled tires.

A space for student design competitions, known as the Bay, gives student teams a place to build projects of all kinds—from drones and autonomous robots to automobiles and even submarines.

Royal Society

UBC faculty are frequently honoured with international awards that highlight their contributions to teaching and research. The Royal Society—a group of 1,500 leading scientists, engineers and technology innovators—has inducted 11 UBC professors as fellows.

Since 2012, three faculty have been made members of the society:

Recent Members

2017:
Department of Mathematics professor **Gordon Slade** was inducted for his mathematical studies of critical phenomena and phase transitions.

2015:
Natalie Strynadka, professor in the Department of Biochemistry and Molecular Biology, was inducted for her work studying proteins and protein assemblies involved in pathogenic bacteria and antibiotic resistance.

2012:
Department of Chemistry professor **Steve Withers** was inducted for his research on the reaction mechanism of enzymes, which relates to key biological processes such as energy storage and cell wall strength.

National Academies of Sciences, Engineering and Medicine, and National Academy of Inventors

Numerous UBC professors have been honoured in the United States with memberships in the National Academies of Sciences, Engineering and Medicine, and in the National Academy of Inventors.

Inductees in the past 10 years include:

Recent Members

2019:
Margo Seltzer (Computer Science), National Academy of Engineering

2017:
Dolph Schluter (Zoology), National Academy of Sciences

2017:
Marc Parlange (Civil Engineering), National Academy of Engineering

2017:
Pieter Cullis (Biochemistry and Molecular Biology), National Academy of Inventors

2017:
Lorne Whitehead (Physics and Astronomy), National Academy of Inventors

2016:
Terrance Snutch (Neuroscience), National Academy of Inventors

2016:
Philip Hieter (Medical Genetics), National Academy of Sciences

2015:
Edith McGeer (Medicine), National Academy of Inventors

2015:
Patrick McGeer (Medicine), National Academy of Inventors

2014:
Julian Davies (Microbiology and Immunology), National Academy of Sciences

2013:
Sarah (Sally) Otto (Biology), National Academy of Sciences

UBC president **Santa Ono** was also inducted into the National Academy of Inventors in 2013, while he was president and professor of medicine at the University of Cincinnati.

American Academy of Arts and Sciences

The American Academy of Arts and Sciences honours excellence in a variety of fields, recognizing leaders who advance "the interest, honor, dignity and happiness" of society.

Ten UBC professors and administrators have been inducted since 2003:

Inductees

2019:
Candis Callison (School of Journalism)

2016:
Sarah (Sally) Otto (Zoology)

2014:
Janet Werker (Psychology)

2013:
Mike Whitlock (Zoology)

2012:
Philip Hieter (Medical Genetics)

2012:
Dolph Schluter (Zoology)

2007:
Donald Ludwig (Mathematics)

2004:
Loren Rieseberg (Biology)

2003:
Lloyd Axworthy (Liu Institute)

2003:
William Unruh (Physics and Astronomy)

Guggenheim Fellows

Fellowships with the John Simon Guggenheim Memorial Foundation are often offered to "mid-career" researchers, performers and artists who have shown exceptional scholarship or creative ability.

Since 2011, five UBC professors have been honoured with a Guggenheim Fellowship:

Honourees

2017:
Bryan Gick (Linguistics), for his research on the production, perception and biomechanics of human speech

2015:
Michael Doebeli (Mathematics and Zoology), for his world-leading work on mathematical evolutionary biology

2015:
Dominic McIver Lopes (Philosophy), for his writings on art and aesthetics, including his groundbreaking research on interactive computer art

2011:
Sarah (Sally) Otto (Zoology), for her work exploring the evolutionary processes that underlie and generate biodiversity

2011:
Patrick Keeling (Botany), for his research on the biology and molecular evolution of single-celled organisms called protists

above Behind the scenes at the Frederic Wood Theatre.

facing From performance and audiovisuals to props and wardrobe, the Frederic Wood Theatre has provided a venue for student education since the 1960s.

Theatre and Film

You could say the Department of Theatre and Film began as it should: with a touch of drama. In the 1950s successful theatre artist and English Department professor Dorothy Somerset applied to run a "poetry speaking" course. Her request was denied. Not to be put off, Professor Somerset petitioned the university senate to create an entirely new department focused on theatre. The senate granted this more ambitious request, and in 1958 Somerset got her poetry speaking class—and the job of heading the newly formed Theatre Department.

Early productions were held in a converted snack bar. The renowned 400-seat "Freddy Wood" (Frederic Wood) Theatre was built in the early 1960s, named in honour of one of UBC's first English professors and drama instructors.

UBC offered its inaugural film class in 1966, and the department formally became UBC Theatre and Film a quarter-century later.

Today the department is at the forefront of film and theatre programs in Canada. Graduate students publish *Cinephile*, a peer-reviewed journal exploring film, media and culture studies, and the Frederic Wood Theatre remains UBC's hub of theatrical activity, hosting a full season of plays and professional productions.

Graduates include cinematographer Catherine Lutes, comedian and host Gavin Crawford, and scores of artists who garner recognition throughout the world for their ingenuity, insight and excellence.

Centre for Digital Media

The Centre for Digital Media (CDM) is home to the Master of Digital Media program. One of UBC's many collaborations with other higher-education institutions, CDM is a partnership with Simon Fraser University, Emily Carr University of Art + Design and the British Columbia Institute of Technology.

The centre comprises two buildings equipped with interactive labs, an 8,000-square-foot multi-purpose learning space and a 76-room residence at Vancouver's Great Northern Way campus.

The Master of Digital Media program leverages Vancouver's wealth of art and design talent and the region's world-class cluster of companies developing video games, visual effects and animation. Over 16 months, students work with industry partners to develop the knowledge required to build, manage and lead digital media projects.

A broad network of businesses and organizations work with CDM students—including Electronic Arts, Finger Food Studios, Microsoft and SAP—collaborating with them on projects, providing internships and ultimately hiring many of them as new talent.

To date, 95 per cent of graduates from the Master of Digital Media program are working in their chosen fields; almost a third are working in gaming; and 19 start-up companies have been created by graduates.

facing and above
The Centre for Digital Media, a collaboration between UBC and several other institutions, leverages Vancouver's world-class cluster of companies developing video games, animation and visual effects.

above The Khorog, Tajikistan, campus is one of the University of Central Asia (UCA)'s three campuses. UBC's Geography Department began a partnership with UCA in 2017.

UBC Department of Geography and the University of Central Asia

The Geography Department has won international recognition for many of its programs and research efforts, including studies of urban climates, air pollution and global climate change.

Consistently ranked among the top five geography departments in the world, it offers students a lens on the ways that landscapes influence society and public policy—and a chance to think critically about everything from colonialism to river hydrology to refugee migrations.

Study sites range from the Canadian Arctic to the Andes, from Europe to sub-Saharan Africa, from China to Palestine. One notable project is a new partnership with the University of Central Asia (UCA).

Founded in 2000, UCA is a joint creation of the Kyrgyz Republic, Tajikistan, Kazakhstan and His Highness the Aga Khan, created to "promote the social and economic development of Central Asia, particularly its mountain communities."

In 2017 UBC's Geography Department began working with UCA to design almost two dozen courses for its undergraduate Earth and

Environmental Sciences program. UBC professors will also offer professional development support for UCA faculty.

As signatory to the partnership, UBC president Santa Ono spoke of his hope that it would "not only allow UBC to have critical input into the development of new academic programs half a world away, but will also provide UBC instructors with the chance to reflect on their own courses and how they might be improved and adapted to different learning environments."

above Nobel Prize– winning physicist Carl Wieman helped transform the way science is taught at UBC.

Carl Wieman Science Education Initiative and Educational Technology

More than 18,000 UBC students, 40 courses and nine separate departments in the Faculty of Science were part of the Carl Wieman Science Education Initiative (CWSEI). Through a combination of information technologies, peer instruction approaches and other methods, CWSEI transformed the way science is taught at UBC.

Begun in 2007 and completed in 2017, CWSEI's core emphasis was to develop students' complex problem-solving skills, rather than only their ability to memorize facts. One example of a current CWSEI-inspired classroom technique at UBC is the use of "clickers"—wireless personal response systems that can instantly (and anonymously) canvass all students in a classroom for their answers to a question. Only the professor can see the responses, and if too high a percentage of students answer incorrectly, instructors can then explain the concept further or redirect students to discuss it among themselves.

The CWSEI was named for its founder, Nobel Prize–winning physicist Carl Wieman, who has worked to improve science education in classrooms across North America. A former professor in UBC's Department of Physics and Astronomy, Wieman has served as associate director of the White House Office of Science and Technology Policy and as founding chair of the National Academy of Sciences Board on Science Education.

A study in the journal *Science* analyzed the CWSEI approach to classroom learning and found that it was nearly twice as effective as traditional science education methods.

UBC has a history of using technology to pioneer new approaches to educational delivery. While a member of the Computer Science faculty in the mid-1990s, Murray Goldberg created WebCT, the world's first learning management system (LMS). Goldberg left UBC to run WebCT, which was embraced not only by UBC but also by 4,000 other universities and colleges across the world, serving millions of students in 80 countries. WebCT was absorbed into new software, Blackboard (later Connect). UBC currently runs on the Canvas LMS platform.

More recently, the university has delivered a diverse array of massive open online courses (MOOCs) on everything from water security to forestry to game theory—the last attracting 130,000 registrants in 183 countries. UBC was the first Canadian charter member of edX, which provides MOOCs from such institutions as MIT, the University of California and Harvard, among many others.

Nobel Laureates

UBC has been a place of learning and teaching for eight Nobel laureates. Perhaps best known is Michael Smith, whose genomics work at UBC in the 1970s—specifically a revolutionary process he invented for catalyzing DNA mutations—led to his Nobel Prize in Chemistry in 1993.

As of this writing in 2019, Smith is joined by seven other UBC faculty and graduates who have earned this global honour.

Honourees

Academic staff at time of award:
1993: Michael Smith (Chemistry)

Graduates:
1999: Robert A. Mundell (Economic Sciences)

1994: Bertram N. Brockhouse (Physics)

Academic staff prior to award:
2017: Richard H. Thaler (Economic Sciences)

2002: Daniel Kahneman (Economic Sciences)

1989: Hans G. Dehmelt (Physics)

1968: H. Gobind Khorana (Physiology or Medicine)

Academic staff after award:
2001: Carl Wieman (Physics)

above UBC president Martha C. Piper (left) and Chancellor Allan McEachern (right), met with Nobel Peace Prize winners (left to right) the Dalai Lama, Archbishop Desmond Tutu and Shirin Ebadi in a 2004 visit.

A Trio of Peace Prize Winners

In 2004 UBC was honoured with a visit by three winners of the Nobel Peace Prize: Iranian human rights activist Shirin Ebadi, who won the award in 2003; His Holiness the Dalai Lama of Tibet, who won the prize in 1989; and Archbishop Desmond Tutu of South Africa, awarded the prize in 1984.

The three luminaries travelled to Vancouver at the invitation of Pitman Potter, then director of UBC's Institute of Asian Research, and his colleague Victor Chan. Each of the three Nobel laureates was presented with an honorary Doctor of Laws degree.

As the *Globe and Mail* said of the trio's visit, it was "a one-of-a-kind traveling road show, and we may never see its likes again."

Ethnographic Film Unit

From chronicling the obsession with basketball in Indigenous villages on British Columbia's north coast to delving into traditional family fishing practices in Ireland, the Ethnographic Film Unit (EFU) produces documentaries that link participating communities and anthropology with explorations of social and ecological sustainability.

One of several faculty-run labs within the Department of Anthropology, the EFU is overseen by Charles Menzies, an anthropology professor from Gitxaala Nation. The unit creates traditional narrative documentaries as well as community videos and short vignettes.

One EFU project, *Basketball Warriors*, tells the stories of basketball players from Gitxaala Nation—located south of Prince Rupert on Dolphin Island—and the history and significance of the game on the north coast. Part of the narrative encompasses the BC All Native Basketball Tournament in Prince Rupert, held since 1960.

The hands-on Ethnographic Film Methods course has been taught several times by EFU members. Collaborative student teams have produced short videos, released on DVD or via online video portals, on topics ranging from gardening to performance to political activism.

above Documentaries by the Ethnographic Film Unit—like this one chronicling the passion for basketball on BC's north coast—link participating communities with anthropological explorations.

School of Music

Since it was established in 1947, UBC's School of Music has grown into western Canada's largest university music department. Today, more than 450 students hone their gifts in performance, composition and music scholarship and take part in a wide variety of ensembles—including, among others, two concert bands, five choirs,

a 110-member symphony orchestra, a Balinese gamelan group and an opera company. They perform regularly at the Chan Centre and the Roy Barnett Recital Hall on the Vancouver campus.

Many graduates have gone on to international musical careers as performers, producers and scholars. Pianist James Parker, founding member of chamber music ensemble the Gryphon Trio, has won several Juno Awards; experimental composer and producer Hildegard Westerkamp pioneered the field of sound ecology and has blazed a trail for women in music; internationally renowned tenor (and CBC Radio host) Ben Heppner has led a long career as one of the world's foremost opera singers; and composer Alexina Louie has received many awards throughout her long career, including being named Composer of the Year by the Canadian Music Council.

UBC has long-running relationships with the Vancouver Symphony Orchestra (VSO), Early Music Vancouver, the Vancouver Opera and many other local collaborators. With these partners, the School of Music has launched the Baroque Orchestra Mentorship Program, which trains aspiring Early Music performers, as well as the Summer Music Institute and the UBC Chamber Orchestra Festival.

In 2019 the School of Music co-hosted the VSO Orchestral Institute (VSOI)—an orchestral training institute attracting 100 young, professional-track musicians from around the world. The VSOI stages a concerto competition and recitals and performs chamber music around the city.

facing UBC students have been honing their gifts in performance, composition and music scholarship at the School of Music since 1947.

above Award-winning dramatic tenor Ben Heppner graduated from the UBC School of Music in 1979.

ALUMNI

Ben Heppner

Considered one of the greatest dramatic tenors in the world, Ben Heppner graduated with a degree in music from UBC in 1979—the same year he gained national recognition for winning the CBC Talent Festival.

Heppner debuted at the Metropolitan Opera in *Idomeneo* in 1991, and he went on to become an audience favourite at the Met. Throughout his decades-long career he has performed from Vienna to San Francisco in the world's most prestigious concert and opera halls, and worked with some of the biggest names in the conducting world, including Sir Georg Solti, Wolfgang Sawallisch and Seiji Ozawa.

Heppner has been honoured with an International Emmy, two Grammy Awards for Best Opera Recording, and two Juno Awards. He holds honorary degrees from seven Canadian colleges and universities, including UBC. Since his retirement from the stage in 2014, Heppner has been the weekly host of CBC Radio's *Saturday Afternoon at the Opera* and *Backstage with Ben Heppner.*

SCARP and Indigenous Community Planning

Recognizing the part that community planners have played in the colonization of Indigenous peoples, and to meet the need for planners

who have been exposed to Indigenous approaches to development, in 2012 UBC's School of Community and Regional Planning (SCARP) partnered with the Musqueam people on a new and innovative program.

Many mainstream planners are ill-equipped to engage with First Nations communities, whose paradigms and procedures differ from common Western practices. Indigenous community planning (ICP) is a master's degree specialization that is trying to turn that trend around, with financial support from the Real Estate Foundation of BC and Indigenous Services Canada.

SCARP accepts 10 interested students into the specialization each year, giving them knowledge and tools that will help them support Indigenous communities in achieving their own goals for culturally sustainable development. ICP enrollees are required to complete

left Aviva Rathbone and Morgan Guerin share Musqueam's planning history with first year ICP students at the community's archaeological dig.

right Shauna Johnson and Kelsey Taylor, who completed their ICP practicum with Tla'amin Nation together, celebrate their graduation in 2016.

EXCELLENCE IN TEACHING AND LEARNING

facing The Robson Square campus brings UBC into the heart of downtown Vancouver.

four extra core courses, an internship of 80 to 100 hours with an Indigenous organization and an eight-month practicum working on comprehensive community planning with a First Nations community in British Columbia.

The Musqueam community provides ongoing insight and expertise in the design and delivery of ICP. They were natural partners for the program, and not only for their long relationship with UBC: the band has received global praise for its own Comprehensive Community Plan, which in 2013 was recognized as a best practice plan for sustainable development by UN-Habitat.

Both the partnership and the cultural immersion requirement are unique among North American post-secondary planning programs. Students graduating with the ICP concentration have gone on to work for organizations such as Vancouver Coastal Health and the First Nations Health Authority, and for Indigenous communities in a variety of roles, including lands and resources managers, community planners and engagement coordinators.

Robson Square and the Learning Exchange

When UBC committed to creating classroom and event spaces in Vancouver's downtown core, university leaders chose Robson Square. The Arthur Erickson–designed complex is built like a skyscraper laid

on its side—with the Law Courts at one end and the Vancouver Art Gallery at the other—and was awarded the American Society of Landscape Architects' President's Award of Excellence in 1979.

UBC Robson Square opened in 2001 and now encompasses 81,000 square feet of classroom, meeting and office spaces for a number of programs and departments—including the Sauder School of Business, Extended Learning and Innovation UBC.

The space allows UBC to spark creativity and innovation beyond campus. More than 2,900 events are held annually in its meeting facilities, computer lab and 175-seat theatre.

facing UBC's Creative Writing program has shaped and inspired generations of authors, poets and screenwriters.

UBC also engages with the broader Vancouver community via the Learning Exchange. Located in the Downtown Eastside—one of Canada's poorest neighbourhoods—and staffed by student volunteers, it has provided local residents with drop-in activities and educational programs year-round since 1999. The free courses offered to community members include beginner computer and technology workshops, English as a second language and art workshops.

The life and purpose of the Learning Exchange is summed up in its name: a shared space where community members and the university can exchange experience and expertise; a place where, as the Learning Exchange itself puts it, "everyone has something to teach and something to learn."

Journalism and Creative Writing

Through its Creative Writing program and the Graduate School of Journalism, UBC has long been a magnet for attracting and nurturing the talents of young writers and storytellers.

As one of just four master's-only journalism programs in North America, the Graduate School of Journalism is a training ground for the next generation of media innovators. An undergraduate degree is a prerequisite for new students, as is an interest in learning about a range of formats—print, audio, video, web production and other media—to tell stories and shift public conversations.

The school is modelled on the approach of a small liberal arts college, with small class sizes, an emphasis on fieldwork, and one-on-one contact with faculty. Core instructors are experienced in everything from media studies and public policy journalism to environmental reporting and digital media. Adjunct faculty include award-winning instructors like film journalist Peter Klein, veteran urban affairs reporter Frances Bula, and Anishinaabe author, broadcast journalist and current host of CBC's *Cross Country Checkup*, Duncan McCue.

Faculty and staff mentor on freelancing opportunities and career development, while a required 12-week internship has seen UBC students placed at the *New York Times*, the *Jerusalem Post*, CNN and many Canadian print and broadcast news outlets. The school's International Reporting Program has won multiple awards for its multimedia work, including the Edward R. Murrow Award, an EPPY Award and numerous Canadian Online Publishing Awards.

For writers interested in other forms, UBC's Creative Writing program—founded in 1963 and now one of the largest and most comprehensive writing programs in the world—offers undergraduate and graduate degrees with a "literary cross-training approach." Students study creative nonfiction, fiction, poetry, screenplays, Indigenous writing and more. Recently developed courses have focused on emergent forms, teaching students how to write graphic novels, podcasts and video game scripts.

Students in the Creative Writing program manage and edit UBC's acclaimed literary magazine *PRISM international*, and have received mentoring from award-winning faculty like Susan Musgrave, Timothy Taylor and Annabel Lyon. Graduates have won numerous awards and include writers such as Eden Robinson, Shauna Singh Baldwin, Amy Stuart and Morris Panych.

above Novelist and short-story writer Eden Robinson, who earned her MFA in creative writing at UBC, has won many awards for her work.

ALUMNI

Eden Robinson

Eden Robinson is an award-winning author and graduate of UBC's Master of Fine Arts program in Creative Writing. A novelist and short-story writer of Haisla and Heiltsuk heritage, her first novel, *Monkey Beach*, was shortlisted for both the Scotiabank Giller Prize and a Governor General's Literary Award in 2000. She is the recipient of the 2016 Writers' Trust Engel Findley Award, and her most recent work, *Son of a Trickster*, was shortlisted for the 2017 Scotiabank Giller Prize.

"Mostly I enjoyed the company of people focused on the same goal as me," said Robinson of her experience at UBC. "I found it inspiring, even as I found the learning curve daunting. I was fortunate enough to have mentors that guided me and nurtured me."

In recognition of her literary contributions, Robinson received an honorary doctorate from UBC in 2018.

William Gibson

A graduate of UBC's Department of English, class of 1977, William Gibson is the author of several award-winning science fiction stories and novels, among other works. His 1984 book *Neuromancer* swept the sci-fi triple crown—winning the Hugo, Nebula and Philip K. Dick awards—and launched the cyberpunk genre that is still a part of literary culture today.

Born in South Carolina in 1948, Gibson moved to Canada during the tumultuous years of the 1960s, and after spending several years in Toronto, he and his wife moved to British Columbia. He enrolled at UBC, where a creative writing class encouraged Gibson to try his hand at science fiction.

Upon graduation, he took it seriously as his creative direction—in the process irrevocably changing the genre with his penchant for digital technology and gritty subcultures.

"In 1977, facing first-time parenthood and an absolute lack of enthusiasm for anything like 'career,' I found myself dusting off my 12-year-old self's interest in science fiction," he wrote in an autobiographical essay. "Simultaneously, weird noises were being heard from New York and London. I took Punk to be the detonation of some slow-fused projectile buried deep in society's flank a decade earlier, and I took it to be, somehow, a sign. And I began, then, to write."

Gibson was inducted into the Science Fiction Hall of Fame in 2008, and in 2019 he was named by the Science Fiction and Fantasy Writers of America as the 35th Damon Knight Grand Master in recognition of "lifetime achievement in science fiction and/or fantasy."

Indian Residential School History and Dialogue Centre and Indigenous Educational Opportunities

After a 2011 Truth and Reconciliation Commission of Canada conference on "institutions of memory," UBC's First Nations House of Learning and the Indian Residential School Survivors Society began discussing creating a space that would address and preserve the experiences of west coast survivors of Indian residential schools. The Indian Residential School History and Dialogue Centre opened in April 2018 in a newly built space on the Vancouver campus.

The multi-purpose space has been designed to offer an accessible place for survivors of residential schools—along with their families and communities—to view historical materials gathered by the Truth and Reconciliation Commission and others, and to talk about their experiences.

For those who are not themselves survivors or directly connected to those who lived through the tragic history of residential schooling of First Nations children in Canada, the Indian Residential School History and Dialogue Centre is also a hub for education—as a repository of memory, but also as a proactive generator of advanced curricular materials for university and K–12 students in British Columbia and beyond.

As the centre notes: "It is still very much the case that many students, and most Canadians and other visitors, have had access to no real information about Indigenous people or the history of the interactions that have shaped our country. We have consistently found, however, that even with introductory information about the residential schools and associated matters, students and others are in a much better position to think about their relationships with Indigenous people and the contemporary issues that define our country."

The Indian Residential School History and Dialogue Centre complements ongoing efforts by UBC to provide educational content, spaces and modes of learning that support Indigenous students. Over 1,200 scholars of Indigenous heritage now study at UBC, which has one of the largest concentrations of Indigenous professors of any large research university.

The Aboriginal Centre at UBC Okanagan provides a "home away from home," along with services intended to enrich Indigenous students' university experience. Offerings include peer mentor programs,

cultural activities, academic advising and connections with Indigenous professors.

UBC Okanagan also partners with the En'owkin Centre—a "cultural, educational, ecological and creative arts organization" run by the Okanagan Nation Alliance and located on the Penticton Indian Band reserve—on the Aboriginal Access Studies program, which allows Indigenous students who are not registered with the university to study university-level courses, giving them the ability to upgrade skills and experience university life.

On the Vancouver campus, the First Nations Longhouse has been a hub for coordinating Indigenous education and services since 1993. Built to echo traditional Northwest Coast architecture, the Longhouse is the home of the First Nations House of Learning, which oversees Indigenous initiatives at UBC and provides a point of contact for First Nations communities. It also houses the Faculty of Education's Indigenous Teacher Education Program, which prepares people of Indigenous ancestry to work as teachers, and the X̱wi7x̱wa Library, the only dedicated Indigenous university library in Canada.

UBC Connects

In 2018 UBC president Santa Ono began hosting a public lecture series with leading thinkers, artists and researchers. Part of President Ono's passion for connecting the university to the world at large,

above and facing
Several UBC programs offer students the chance to learn in new environments far from British Columbia, including Sweden (above) and China (facing).

UBC Connects has hosted luminaries from a wide array of disciplines, from futurist Jeremy Rifkin and author Isabel Allende to physicist Michio Kaku and civil rights activist Tarana Burke.

UBC Students Abroad

Like many institutions, UBC Vancouver and UBC Okanagan offer students a variety of ways to learn abroad. Together, they annually provide $1.4 million in financial assistance for students who take up the challenge and opportunity of living in a different country.

Immersion in another culture equips students with fresh perspectives and builds independence, initiative and adaptability—significant traits that not only enhance their personal lives, but their professional trajectory as well.

"To actually take the initiative to leave your home country, your university, and go thousands of miles away, demonstrates something about your grit and your ability to face different situations and to thrive," UBC president Santa Ono said in a 2016 interview. "That is probably the strongest indicator of future success, even more than one's academic performance. It's an incredibly powerful experience. And it's something that's long-lasting."

The Department of French, Hispanic and Italian Studies sponsors courses for UBC students in many locations—including Quebec City,

Venice and Quito—while the Go Global initiative has assisted more than 22,000 UBC students in overseas study through a variety of pathways.

Students can opt for a semester or more at one of 200 partner universities in over 40 countries, or they can take a global seminar. These on-site learning experiences are taught by UBC professors all over the world. Seminars vary in length and intensity, but they all offer students an unforgettable learning experience on topics such as food systems in Italy or the history of World War II in Poland.

UBC's partnerships with other international learning organizations also give students international opportunities to attend conferences, competitions and special programs. A 2019 example is the one-week, fully funded undergraduate student forum that has evolved from UBC's connection with Punjabi University Patiala (PUP) in India. UBC and PUP students jointly take classes, explore the area and do original research together centring on an annual theme.

Students from UBC also have the option to participate in the international Green Challenge hosted by the Technical University of Denmark. Competing for prizes from a total award pool amounting to $49,000, students present projects related to sustainability, the environment and climate technology, competing in Copenhagen against other students from across the world.

Life on Campus

above Students at Ponderosa Commons.

facing Aerial view of the Totem Park student residences.

Commons Housing

UBC enrolled roughly 65,000 students in 2018, with over 85 per cent of them attending the Vancouver campus. That's a lot of students who need a place to live. In the past decade the university has added enough beds to offer residences to 11,700 students, giving it the highest number of beds per full-time student in the country. Plans to build space for another 16,000 students are on the books.

Putting up buildings chock full of beds is relatively easy. Making spaces that actually work well for the academic, social and physical well-being of students—many of whom are far from home, some for the first time—takes some consideration. In recent years UBC has adopted a model successfully used at other universities in North America and beyond: "the commons."

Commons residences are integrated, multi-use spaces that offer students more than a place to sleep and a closet for their clothes. Along with residences and food facilities, commons complexes can offer fitness facilities, study spaces, classrooms, faculty offices and child care centres—along with surrounding public areas that support active, outdoor lifestyles.

"The idea," said President Santa Ono, "is that a commons facilitates conversations between faculty and students over lunch or coffee, allows for classrooms to be used by resident students for studying throughout the evenings and weekends when classes are not in

above The trend toward "commons" residences—such as Orchard Commons above—offers students a variety of amenities that support healthy lifestyles and community connections.

session, and promotes interdisciplinary learning through exposure to professors and labs outside of a student's home faculty."

So far the university has built three: Brock Commons, Ponderosa Commons and Orchard Commons. As one example, Ponderosa Commons has five residences for upper-year and graduate students. Centrally located and housing 1,150 students, Ponderosa was built in 2013. It now incorporates a fitness facility, two food outlets, the Audain Art Centre's studios and gallery, Faculty of Education classrooms and offices, and a geography lab. There are also two "collegia" offering commuter students places to hang out, study and even take a nap.

"Not surprisingly," said President Ono, "both Ponderosa and Orchard Commons are the residences most desired by students. Unlike our more traditional student residences, these are places that serve the whole campus community."

Holi Fest

What comes dressed in white and leaves looking like a rainbow? The thousand-plus UBC students attending the annual Holi festival presented by the Indian Students' Association.

Held in March, the spring festival is a Hindu tradition celebrating the triumph of good over evil. Delicious Indian food, packets of coloured powder and a good dose of beats by Bollywood DJs give students a way to dance away the stresses of impending final exams.

The Indian Students' Association is one of several student-run campus groups celebrating their heritage cultures. UBC's student body is a diverse group hailing from more than 150 countries, reflecting both the demographics of British Columbia itself and the university's growing reputation worldwide.

above Every spring the Indian Students' Association hosts the popular and colourful Holi festival.

above The traditions and perspectives of international students enrich the UBC campus experience.

Currently there are over 16,000 international students who have travelled to Canada to attend classes on UBC's Vancouver and Okanagan campuses. The top five source countries are, in order, China, the United States, India, Korea and Japan. Students bringing their traditions and perspectives (and beats) from around the world enliven and enrich the campus experience for everyone.

UBC Okanagan Commons

Opened in 2019, the $35-million Commons building is a flagship space for the UBC Okanagan community. Built as an addition to the library—the most intensively used library in the UBC system—it provides a digital design laboratory, a media lab, a video production studio and classrooms. It also offers a wide array of new study spaces, including the 6,400-square-foot D. Ross Fitzpatrick Great Hall.

The project was funded in part by a $10-million infusion from UBC Okanagan students themselves, thanks to a 2014 student-led referendum.

"We are very proud of this legacy, which we leave to future generations of students and to our UBC Okanagan campus," said UBC Okanagan Student Union president Amal Alhuwayshil. "These new spaces open up much-needed study space and inspire collaboration. They support our ability to create world-class projects, right here at UBC Okanagan."

above Built in part with student funds, the new UBC Okanagan Commons building offers a wide array of spaces for conversation, study and research.

above UBC Okanagan graduate Neetu Garcha is an award-winning broadcast journalist and news anchor.

ALUMNI

Neetu Garcha

A first-generation Canadian of Punjabi ancestry, Neetu Garcha is a television, radio and online journalist and news anchor.

The recipient of the Broadcast Performer of Tomorrow award presented by the BC Association of Broadcasters, Garcha's path to journalism started with a business management degree from UBC Okanagan in Kelowna, not far from her family home in Penticton. There she hosted radio shows, got involved with the university's campus television station and became its host and producer.

After completing the journalism program at the British Columbia Institute of Technology, she went on to work for Global News BC, reporting on a wide range of topics and geographies. Garcha has reported from Haiti and covered the 2016 Syrian refugee immigration crisis from Greece. Closer to home, she reported live from Green Party headquarters during their 2017 provincial election breakthrough, and spent almost three weeks that same year tracking the impacts of wildfires across the BC Interior.

"I believe in journalism's power to do good," said Garcha. "I believe that the struggles, scandals and stories of people from all walks of life need to be researched and reported."

Musqueam Signage

UBC's campus map went bilingual in 2018. In partnership with the Musqueam community, nine new street signs in the hən̓q̓əmin̓əm̓ language were placed beside the English versions at 54 spots around the central campus.

The language of hən̓q̓əmin̓əm̓ is traditionally oral rather than written, and it contains 36 consonants, 22 of which don't occur in English. Some can be heard only in a few other languages worldwide. What you see on the campus signs are the specialized symbols of the North American Phonetic Alphabet, which the Musqueam have formally adopted to share and preserve their language.

Some of the new street names function close to translations of their English counterparts. Memorial Road has been named šxʷhək̓ʷmət, a word that means "that which is used to remember" people and events. The word q̓ʷeχt for Agricultural Road was chosen for its meaning of a root plot, garden or orchard.

The language of the Musqueam roots them in their local terrain. West Mall has been named sme:ntásəm, "facing the mountains," for the view as you travel north along it, and the name for Lower Mall is stəywət, which means "west wind"—a description of walking close to the shoreline and feeling the Salish Sea breezes.

above Fifty-four signs in the hən̓q̓əmin̓əm̓ language reflect the deep ties between UBC's Point Grey campus and the Musqueam.

above Hereditary Chief 7idansuu (James Hart) of the Haida Nation, carver of *Reconciliation Pole.*

facing Carved from an 800-year-old cedar, *Reconciliation Pole* depicts the Indigenous experience in Canada before, during and after residential schools.

Reconciliation Pole

Erected on UBC's Main Mall in 2017, *Reconciliation Pole* looks north toward the new Indian Residential School History and Dialogue Centre. The placement is appropriate for the 17-metre pole, which expresses the devastating history of residential schools in Canada and looks toward a better future of healing and harmony.

Reconciliation Pole was carved from an 800-year-old cedar by Haida hereditary Chief and master carver James Hart, also known by his hereditary name 7idansuu (Edenshaw). The symbols Hart incorporated into *Reconciliation Pole*—which in traditional Haida fashion are read from the bottom up—depict the Indigenous experience in Canada before, during and after residential schools.

Residential schools are infamous for their attempt to repress and erase the inherited cultures of children who were forced to attend, and for decades of systemic abuse. Approximately 68,000 copper nails were hammered into the pole to honour and represent the thousands of Indigenous children who died in residential schools.

The base of the pole features traditional Haida imagery representing the sacred wholeness of life, while the centre is carved with an image of an institutional building inspired by the residential school that Hart's own grandfather attended. Among other symbols, the top of the pole shows an eagle spreading its wings to fly, which Hart said represents "the power and determination" needed to move forward.

"My hope for the pole is that it moves people to learn more about the history of residential schools and to understand their responsibility to reconciliation," said Hart. "The schools were terrible places. Working on the pole has been difficult, but I have loved it too. We need to pay attention to the past and work together on a brighter future."

facing The Earth Sciences Building inspires cross-disciplinary innovation while putting science on display.

Earth Sciences Building

The $75-million Earth Sciences Building (ESB) was built in 2012. Laboratories and expanded learning spaces serve the approximately 6,500 students who study earth sciences each year. Located in the midst of the university's science district, the ESB is also home to the Department of Statistics and the Pacific Institute for the Mathematical Sciences.

The structure was designed to inspire cross-disciplinary creativity with a wide variety of meeting spaces. Even the building's staircase— five storeys, cantilevered and made of solid timber—features extra- wide landings to offer space for pauses and conversation as people pass each other en route to offices or classrooms.

Like the Beaty Biodiversity Museum across Main Mall, the ESB was built to put science on display. Its exterior features huge, polished slabs of rock samples, while floor-to-ceiling windows offer passing students and visitors a glimpse into the daily life of earth sciences research at UBC.

Earth, Ocean and Atmospheric Sciences faculty have been recog- nized for a wide array of achievements and groundbreaking analyses. Professor Matthijs Smit's recent work on subduction zones has helped advance global understanding of plate tectonics. Professor Cather- ine Johnson, meanwhile, specializes in the more far-flung field of comparative planetary geophysics—studying the magnetic fields,

earthquakes and lithosphere not only of Earth but also of Mercury, Mars, Venus and the moon. In 2019 Johnson was awarded the Shen Kuo Award for Interdisciplinary Achievements for her contributions to a "holistic understanding" of our solar system.

above Students in the Faculty of Forestry study forestry, wood products processing and natural resource conservation.

Forest Sciences Centre

Forests cover almost two-thirds of British Columbia, so it's fitting that UBC is home to Canada's largest forestry school—and helps lead the world in forestry education and research.

Emerging foresters learn how to responsibly harvest trees in the spectacular setting of the Forest Sciences Centre. Completed in 1998, the centre is now the academic home of almost 90 faculty members and 1,500 students from three forestry departments.

The architecture showcases the form-and-function potential of Canadian forest products in large-scale construction, with its three distinct blocks—a laboratory block, an office block and a wood processing centre—connected by a sweeping atrium lined with Douglas fir and big-leaf maple. The atrium's beams support a skylight roof, inspired by the visual experience of a forest canopy.

UBC has been educating students in forestry since 1918, with a full Faculty of Forestry established in 1951. (In 1957 the department's size got a big boost thanks to an influx of students and staff fleeing Soviet repression in Hungary.) Today, students of the department study forestry, wood products processing and natural resource conservation both locally and internationally.

The faculty has two research forests: the Alex Fraser Research Forest near Williams Lake in the BC Interior, and the Malcolm Knapp Research Forest located near Maple Ridge. These working forests provide an arena for students to apply what they learn in the

classroom—and for researchers to perform studies in forest management, cultivation, harvesting, ecology and conservation.

The faculty also has a stated commitment to ensuring that its courses "accurately represent and include Aboriginal cultures, histories and systems of knowledge, and are relevant to Aboriginal communities and their needs and concerns."

From January to April, the Faculty of Forestry runs the Haida Gwaii Semester in Natural Resource Studies in HlGaagilda (Skidegate) in Haida Gwaii in northern British Columbia. The courses feature local guest speakers and help students consider the social aspects of natural resources management and the vital issues of Indigenous rights and title.

above The Forest Sciences Centre features a striking atrium lined with Douglas fir and big-leaf maple.

above UBC forestry graduate and philanthropist Irving "Ike" Barber helped found many important programs at institutions around British Columbia.

ALUMNI
Irving "Ike" Barber

After leaving high school and serving with the Royal Canadian Air Force in World War II, Irving "Ike" Barber planned to become a forest ranger upon his return to civilian life. But free tuition credits offered to veterans by the government prompted him to attend UBC, where he graduated in 1950 with a Bachelor of Science in Forestry.

This second chance at higher education sparked Barber's long and successful career in the forest industry. After a quarter-century working in the sector, in 1978 he founded Slocan Forest Products at the age of 55, building it into one of North America's leading lumber producers.

His subsequent generosity as a philanthropist led to research programs like UBC's Irving K. Barber Diabetes Research Fund and the Ike Barber Human Islet Transplant Laboratory at Vancouver General Hospital.

His contributions also helped build the Irving K. Barber Learning Centre at UBC Vancouver and the Irving K. Barber School of Arts and Sciences at UBC Okanagan, along with programs at other institutions across the province, from the University of Northern British Columbia to the Justice Institute of British Columbia.

Wander Wood

There's a lot of room on the Vancouver campus for displays, and occasionally student projects show up alongside more permanent sculptures to adorn Main Mall or other spots.

Wander Wood was an installation created as part of a workshop called Robot Made: Large-Scale Robotic Timber Fabrication in Architecture. An eight-axis robot created segments of the ultimate structure, which was intended to test out approaches to computer-programmed, parametric design—an architectural trend currently getting a lot of attention from researchers.

Funded by a grant from UBC's Centre for Advanced Wood Processing, the project was created by students from the School of Architecture and Landscape Architecture along with advisors from the University of Waterloo and Lang Wilson Practice in Architecture Culture.

above The UBC campus offers ample room for students to display innovative projects.

above and facing
The Chan Centre for the Performing Arts attracts the world's most talented artists to its cello-inspired concert hall.

Chan Centre for the Performing Arts

The Chan Centre for the Performing Arts is UBC's renowned musical performance and arts venue, housed in one of the most iconic buildings on the Vancouver campus.

Designed by visionary architect Bing Thom, the performance centre opened in 1997. The venue's centrepiece is the 1,185-seat Chan Shun Concert Hall. Inspired by the shape of a cello, with curved maple walls mimicking the instrument contours, the concert hall is famous for crystal-clear acoustics enhanced by an adjustable, 22-tonne chandelier-style canopy.

Since opening, the Chan Centre has attracted hundreds of luminaries from classical, jazz, opera and world music—performers like Yo-Yo Ma, Wynton Marsalis, Chick Corea and Tanya Tagaq.

above Crystal-clear acoustics in the Chan Shun Concert Hall are enhanced by a chandelier-style canopy.

Students from UBC and beyond benefit from the Chan Centre, and not just as audience members. Eight thousand UBC students from all departments receive their degrees at graduation ceremonies at the Chan Centre each spring and fall. Throughout the year, the venue provides a world-class space for emerging composers, scholars and performers from the UBC School of Music, as well as offering space for film classes and theatre productions by the Department of Theatre and Film.

The Chan Centre is also home to the Roots and Shoots World Music Education Program. Through workshops and live performances by artists such as the Kokoma African Heritage Ensemble, Cheondoong and Aché Brasil, Roots and Shoots engages young people from a variety of socioeconomic and cultural backgrounds in hearing and playing world music.

A Focus on Well-Being

University can be the best time of your life—but the pressure of classes, papers and exams can take a toll on students' well-being. Almost 20 per cent of Canadians experience either a mental health or substance-use issue every year, and young people between the ages of 15 and 24 are more likely to deal with these than any other age group.

UBC is working to design campus residences and an overall environment that ensures students have access to healthy food, physical recreation and outdoor spaces. As an institution, it advocates a "Thrive 5" model for mental health, which encourages students to balance their rigorous academic lifestyle with walking and stretching, getting enough sleep, eating well, volunteering and spending time with family or friends.

In 2015, UBC Okanagan co-hosted the International Conference on Health Promoting Universities and Colleges. Participants from 45 countries contributed, as well as UNESCO and the World Health Organization. This resulted in the Okanagan Charter, which aims to

above and overleaf
UBC offers students a variety of resources to promote mental health and well-being.

LIFE ON CAMPUS

provide institutions with a common language, framework and principles to create campuses that promote health and well-being.

UBC was one of the first institutions to adopt the charter—which has since been signed by institutions throughout the world—and launched the Wellbeing Strategic Framework that same year. The framework is a collaborative effort to make the university a better place to live, work and learn through a systems-wide approach to well-being across both campuses, guided by the Okanagan Charter.

Faculty are advised on ways to detect students who may be in distress, and UBC offers a variety of self-directed resources to support students' psychological and physical well-being, wherever they fall on the emotional spectrum. The Wellness Centre on the Vancouver campus offers the services of trained peer educators, nurses and wellness advisors (master's-trained counsellors) who can confidentially advise students on available resources. Indigenous students can also request Indigenous counsellors and other specialized assistance through the First Nations House of Learning.

At UBC Okanagan, the Interprofessional Clinic has tested a walk-in clinic allowing students to get a mental health checkup without an appointment. A "stepped care" model offers students access to resources for self-reflection, one-on-one counselling, community resources, support groups and workshops.

Students themselves have taken the initiative to promote physical and mental well-being at UBC. Student-supported resources

include peer academic coaches and a one-on-one peer support program called Speakeasy. The AMS-affiliated Mental Health Awareness Club also hosts events throughout the winter term, such as the annual Doggy De-Stress days.

above UBC Okanagan students pet away their worries at a Doggy De-Stress event.

Botanical Garden

UBC Botanical Garden inherited its founding plants from the province over 100 years ago. In 1912 British Columbia began a botanical garden near New Westminster, under the direction of its first provincial botanist, John Davidson. When his funding was pulled four years later, Davidson and three colleagues saved the collection by transporting thousands of plants, truckload by truckload, over the bumpy roads to UBC's Point Grey campus.

Initially intended for studying British Columbia's native flora, the Botanical Garden has blossomed into a lush environment where students and visitors can observe plants from all over the world. About

Over a hundred years in the making, UBC's Botanical Garden is an oasis featuring over 120,000 plant varieties.

above The Roseline Sturdy Amphitheatre in the garden is a popular location for weddings and performances.

120,000 plants thrive in the Asian, Alpine, BC Rainforest, Garry Oak and Physic gardens. It preserves significant collections of magnolia, maple and ash trees, along with rhododendrons and climbing plants.

The Harold and Frances Holt Physic Garden, oriented around a central sundial, is an homage to the early botanical gardens that educated physicians and apothecaries in the art of making cures—some more successful than others—from plants.

Another highlight is the Nitobe Memorial Garden, a Japanese "tea and stroll garden," considered one of the most authentic of its kind outside of Japan. Dedicated to agriculturist and diplomat Inazo Nitobe, the garden opened in 1960. Imported maple, cherry and azaleas share the garden with native BC species that have been pruned and trained in the traditional tea garden style. Each of the garden's elements, from the plants to the stones, has been carefully placed to symbolize the harmony of natural forces.

Features like the Nitobe, Garry Oak and Physic gardens attract over 100,000 visitors to the Botanical Garden each year. They are also a vital part of UBC's biodiversity collections, used throughout the year for education, conservation and research.

An Imperial Visit

In 2009 Emperor Akihito and Empress Michiko of Japan visited UBC on the last portion of their 11-day tour of Canada.

"I am in Japan!" said the Emperor while walking around Nitobe Memorial Garden. It was the second time the Emperor has visited UBC—the first time was in 1953, when he was still Crown Prince.

above Emperor Akihito and Empress Michiko of Japan visited Nitobe Memorial Garden in 2009.

LIFE ON CAMPUS

above Cold winter temperatures can't keep the *"Tuum Est!"* spirit down—even at the beach.

Polar Bear Swim

There's something slightly crazy about diving into the Pacific Ocean in late November—but then, periods of deranged behaviour can be crucial to surviving the academic year.

At UBC, a clean-up of Wreck Beach precedes the Polar Bear Swim, an annual rite celebrating the end of the fall semester. Despite ocean temperatures that hover around 8°C, in 2018 about 850 UBC students took the plunge.

Snowball Fights

Vancouver doesn't get a lot of snow. When the white stuff really dumps, UBC students tend to make the most of it, as they did at this epic snowball fight in 2019.

above If you're walking down Main Mall after a big snowstorm, watch out.

above and facing The Engineers' Cairn has been a campus monument—and a target—for over 50 years.

The Engineers' Cairn

The Engineers' Cairn became a UBC monument not through careful planning or design, but simply because UBC's engineering students just … put it there. And not just once.

In 1966 and 1968, the Engineering Undergraduate Society (EUS) built two unofficial monuments honouring "the diversified and continuing contributions to campus life by the Engineers." Each monument was dismantled by the university soon after.

In 1969 a new tribute, a white Engineers' Cairn with red, block-letter *E*'s stamped on each of its three sides, was erected. The cairn was rumoured to be reinforced with a cage of steel rebar, which would make it difficult to remove or destroy—and so it remained.

Later that year, however, the university unveiled plans for the new Sedgewick Undergraduate Library. The cairn was right in the middle of the proposed site. Rather than destroy another engineering monument, the EUS hired a crane to move the cairn to its current location by the MacLeod Building.

The Engineers' Cairn stood until 1988 when students from the Faculty of Forestry—the engineers' long-time rivals—attacked it with a backhoe equipped with a pneumatic drill. They then used the cairn's rubble to spell *FORESTRY* on the lawn. (The forestry students, apparently, found none of the legendary rebar.) With the help of engineering graduates, a new two-and-a-half-metre cairn was rebuilt in its place with a concrete foundation and, yes, a cage of reinforcing rebar. The cairn was christened in 1989 by smashing a bottle of beer on its corner.

Still in place today, the rebuilt monument is a constant target: it has become a tradition for groups to paint or redecorate the cairn, which always gets repainted in its original white and red. In November and December every year, the cairn is painted with a rose and affixed with a rare "Do Not Paint" sign. The rose honours the 14 female engineering students who were killed in the 1989 École Polytechnique massacre.

The cairn is such a widely known campus icon that in 2018, engineering student and former EUS president Alan Ehrenholz—whose father and grandfather were also EUS members—ran for Alma Mater Society president, with his name appearing on the ballot as "The Engineers' Cairn."

On social media on election day, a student asked, "Did anyone else literally just vote for a giant hunk of concrete?" Another student quipped, "Yup, cuz none of the other candidates have a concrete platform." Ehrenholz won.

facing Volkswagen Beetles have long been a calling card for pranks by the Engineering Undergraduate Society.

Engineering Pranks

The elaborate and technically harrowing pranks staged by UBC engineering students over the decades have become the stuff of legend. The tradition was taken to new heights in February 2001, when the city of San Francisco woke to find a Volkswagen Beetle suspended from the Golden Gate Bridge—a Canadian flag painted on one side, an *E* for UBC Engineering on the other.

This prankster tradition of the Engineering Undergraduate Society (EUS) has its origins in the mists of UBC time. While engineering students neither confirm nor deny their involvement in most of the exploits of which they've been accused, documented accounts of their hijinks date to at least the 1950s. In 1952 they attempted to kidnap the president of the Nursing Undergraduate Society, and when their failed attempt was mocked by writers at *The Ubyssey*, they kidnapped (not for the first time) later-to-be-famous journalist Allan Fotheringham—and chained him to the Birks clock pole at Georgia and Granville in downtown Vancouver.

Volkswagen Beetles have long been a calling card for EUS pranks. In 2008 one mysteriously appeared suspended below the Lions Gate Bridge. In 1980, and again in 2014, a single Beetle was stranded on top of UBC's clock tower next to Koerner Plaza. (Also in 2014, Engineering dean Marc Parlange arrived at work one morning to discover his office had been converted into a fully stocked janitor's closet.)

Not all of the pranks have been a success: a plan to suspend the body of a V W Bug from Vancouver's Ironworkers Memorial Bridge in 2009 ended in police catching the students "red-handed" when the cable snapped and the car plunged into Burrard Inlet. There were no injuries, fortunately, except to the egos of the five students who perhaps needed some remedial courses in physics and materials engineering.

The Nest

The Nest is the central hub of UBC student life on the Vancouver campus. Five storeys high and encompassing almost 250,000 square feet, it offers students an abundance of places to eat, study and socialize. Built around a vast central atrium, the Nest includes an art gallery and a climbing wall.

It's also home to the latest incarnation of the Pit Pub, a hangout and event venue whose origins can be traced to a 1968 opinion piece—succinctly titled "What This Campus Needs Is a Pub"—written by a then little-known associate professor of zoology named David Suzuki.

Completed in 2015, the $106-million building—constructed to LEED Platinum standards of environmental design—was made

possible by an $85-million contribution from the UBC Alma Mater Society (AMS).

The AMS is the university's student society, whose elected leaders have been advocating for the university's students since 1915. If any campus organization embodies the work-hard, play-hard philosophy of UBC, it's the AMS. It connects students to tutoring, affordable health coverage and campus safety initiatives, while also acting as a social convenor: the AMS hosts dozens of events, from live music shows like the Block Party to competitions like the annual Faculty Cup.

facing and above
At almost 250,000 square feet, the Nest offers students and their clubs a wide variety of places to eat, read and meet with friends.

above, facing and overleaf With roots going back to the early 20th century, *The Ubyssey* and CiTR continue to be a vital part of student life.

The Ubyssey and CiTR

Since 1918, *The Ubyssey* has been UBC's source for campus political, entertainment and sporting news. Past contributors include Pierre Berton, who once admitted he was more interested in working for the paper than attending class, and future Canadian prime minister John Turner, who edited the sports section in his student years.

A parade of editors and writers has appeared in its pages through the decades. With their influence, *The Ubyssey* has veered from liberal to conservative and from parody to punditry. It has often been a progressive voice, pushing hot buttons with outspoken op-eds as far back as the mid-1950s. When editorials in that era criticized McCarthyism and denounced anti-Semitism and intolerance, the newspaper was described by a professor at Assumption College as "the vilest rag you can imagine, and the best argument for censorship that could be produced."

Loved or hated, *The Ubyssey* endures as a vital forum for information, entertainment and hashing out occasional campus controversies.

Its cousin in this respect is UBC's own radio station, now called CiTR. The inspiration for a campus radio station goes back to 1937, in a time when students desperate for music took to playing records on a gramophone in the university cafeteria. When plans for a university station were announced that year, broadcasting over the airwaves was a recent phenomenon, and the CBC itself was less than a year old.

After successfully launching in the pre-war era, the station went through many incarnations, eventually broadcasting as CiTR on AM radio in 1974. It made the switch to the FM dial in the early 1980s and is now operated by the Student Radio Society of UBC—broadcasting over 100 shows in seven languages, streaming content online and producing podcasts.

Along with publishing the newsprint magazine *Discorder* on music and culture, the station is well known for launching the career of music journalist and Canadian cultural icon Nardwuar the Human Serviette. Over the last 30 years, the inimitable Nardwuar—always clad in his signature plaid tam—has employed an offbeat, research-intensive interviewing style to impress, frustrate and baffle guests as diverse as Nirvana, Jay-Z, Iggy Pop and Jean Chrétien.

Block Party

Have you been to an outdoor concert with 6,000 of your closest friends? That's the AMS Block Party. Held on UBC's Vancouver campus every year to celebrate the last day of classes, this now-classic event has been part of campus culture since 2008.

The Alma Mater Society (AMS) hosts the huge celebration to commemorate another year of learning and give students a chance to let loose. Festivities include seven hours of live music, dancing and games, with a fleet of local food trucks providing the calories. Past acts include Mother Mother, K'naan, Adventure Club, Shad and electronic music DJ and producer Ekali.

above The academic year ends with a blast, if not a bang, at the annual AMS Block Party.

Research
and
Innovation

facing The Canadian Hydrogen Intensity Mapping Experiment (CHIME) can scan huge areas of the sky, creating a three-dimensional map of cosmic hydrogen density.

Thirty Meter Telescope and CHIME

UBC astronomy and astrophysics researchers are poised for new discoveries, thanks to the advent of two new telescopes—each the largest and most powerful of its kind. One is in the midst of being built on Mauna Kea in Hawaii and is expected to begin operation in 2027; the other is already gathering data from its location in British Columbia and making news around the world.

Named for the massive size of its primary mirror, the Thirty Meter Telescope on Mauna Kea will be one of a handful of extremely large telescopes in the world. Canada is a major partner in the project, having contributed $243 million toward construction.

UBC astronomy professor Paul Hickson served as co-chair of the project's science advisory committee as well as a member of its review panel. Hickson wrote that the Thirty Meter Telescope will be "the world's most advanced large-aperture optical/infrared telescope," able to achieve resolutions 10 times greater than the Hubble Space Telescope.

"Its combination of a 30-metre aperture and adaptive optics," said Hickson, "will make it 100 times more sensitive than the largest current telescopes, opening new scientific frontiers."

The Canadian Hydrogen Intensity Mapping Experiment (CHIME) is already making groundbreaking discoveries. The result of a collaboration between over 50 researchers—led by UBC, the Perimeter Institute, the University of Toronto, McGill University and the

National Research Council of Canada—CHIME looks more like a skateboard attraction than a traditional telescope. Unlike traditional dish reflectors, the $16-million radio signal array is constructed of four stationary 20-by-100-metre reflectors that allow it to scan huge areas of the sky.

CHIME will create a three-dimensional map of cosmic hydrogen density that will help researchers measure the universe's history of expansion—and hopefully understand more about the nature of dark matter and why expansion is accelerating rather than slowing down. Along the way it will also provide new data on pulsars and fast radio bursts.

In early 2019, after only two weeks in operation, CHIME caught global attention when it discovered one of only two "repeating" fast radio bursts ever recorded.

"The findings are just the beginning of CHIME's discoveries," said UBC astrophysicist and CHIME team member Ingrid Stairs. "In the next phase, we plan to capture the full high-resolution data stream from the brightest bursts, which will let us better understand their positions, characteristics and magnetic environments. The next few years will be very exciting."

Robert Langlands

In mathematics, you may be fairly certain of your stature when entire areas of study are named for you. This is true for the man behind the Langlands group, the Langlands-Shahidi method and the Langlands program—"a kind of grand unified theory of mathematics," in the words of renowned mathematician Edward Frenkel. The Langlands program has drawn hundreds of researchers into the new fields of study it has opened up.

That man is Robert Langlands. His unifying theory was originally formulated in a letter to a colleague, in which he wrote: "If you are willing to read it as pure speculation I would appreciate that. If not—I am sure you have a waste basket handy."

His ideas didn't end up in the garbage; instead, they propelled him to his current status as one of the leading mathematicians of the 20th century.

Born in New Westminster, BC, in 1936, Langlands earned his degree in mathematics at UBC in 1957, and his master's there only a year later. (He obtained his PhD from Yale University in a scant two years.) He went on to teach at Yale and at Princeton, and he is currently an emeritus professor at the latter's Institute for Advanced Study.

The American Mathematical Society commended his "revolutionary" work with a prize in 1988. As it turned out, this was only the start of a long winning streak. In 1996 his "path-blazing" work

was recognized with the prestigious Wolf Prize; in 2007 he shared the US$1-million Shaw Prize with UK mathematics genius Richard Taylor; and in 2018 he received the Abel Prize from the Norwegian Academy of Science and Letters. The prize, presented to him by His Majesty King Harald V, is worth approximately C$900,000.

UBC Okanagan Researchers of the Year

UBC professors have a history of changing their communities—and the world—in ways that reach beyond their classroom and research duties. UBC Okanagan recognizes these professors and the impacts they make with its annual Researcher of the Year Award.

Barbara Pesut

A professor of nursing in the Faculty of Health and Social Development at UBC Okanagan, Barbara Pesut is part of a team focused on enhancing end-of-life care for underserved populations. Her work learning about the needs and experiences of palliative care patients and their families in rural areas is helping boost resources for such care in the BC Interior and other regions across Canada.

Nancy Holmes

Creative writing professor Nancy Holmes helps lead Border Free Bees, an organization that has encouraged hundreds of people and organizations in Kelowna to learn about bees and provide habitat for them

top Barbara Pesut, UBC Okanagan Health Researcher of the Year for 2018.

bottom Nancy Holmes, UBC Social Sciences and Humanities Researcher of the Year for 2018.

facing The Cascadia Urban Analytics Cooperative uses data on health, housing and transportation to help build better cities.

on public lands and in their own backyards. The project received international recognition in 2017, with Holmes and her associate, Cameron Cartiere, honoured with the National Pollinator Advocate Award from the North American Pollinator Protection Campaign.

Shahria Alam

In British Columbia alone, the cost of repairing damage from a 9.0-magnitude earthquake has been estimated at close to $75 billion. Engineering professor Shahria Alam is developing smarter, safer and greener construction materials and systems that help to prevent the collapse of buildings, bridges and other infrastructure—not only in British Columbia, but in earthquake-prone areas around the world.

Cascadia Urban Analytics Cooperative

The world is increasingly urban, and cities face complex challenges as their populations continue to grow. The Cascadia Urban Analytics Cooperative is a research partnership between UBC and the University of Washington focused on addressing these issues.

The cooperative translates vast data about cities in the region between Vancouver and Portland—a cross-border area known informally as "Cascadia"—into collective action on housing, transportation, health and the environment.

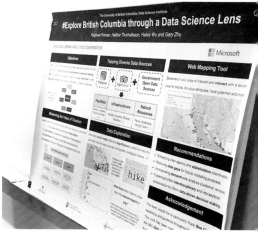

One example is the Neighborhood Change Project, which investigates data on racial and socioeconomic differences in a variety of categories—including housing, poverty and health—in the rapidly expanding cities of Seattle, Vancouver and Surrey.

The multidisciplinary effort uses sociology and urban analytics, among other approaches, to better understand the ways that changes in neighbourhoods affect individuals and families.

The cooperative defines itself as "an applied, interdisciplinary, regional center that brings together academic researchers, students, and public stakeholder groups." The University of Washington is represented by the UW eScience Institute, Urbanalytics and Urban@UW, while UBC brings support from the Data Science Institute and the Sustainability Initiative.

above UBC is a global leader in health, genomics and infectious disease research.

Medical Research

As one of the leading research universities in the world, UBC attracts top scholars who are advancing their disciplines to improve health outcomes around the world.

Dr. Julio Montaner is one of the many researchers who have put UBC on the map for medical excellence. Montaner came to UBC from Buenos Aires as a postdoctoral fellow in 1981; after completing his residency, he went on to join the faculty at St. Paul's Hospital/UBC as the director of the AIDS Research Program and the Infectious Disease Clinic. There Montaner played a critical role in establishing the use of highly active antiretroviral therapy (HAART) in the treatment of HIV/AIDS.

HAART became the new global standard of care in the mid-1990s, and Montaner then focused on bringing it to hard-to-reach populations, including users of intravenous drugs. He pioneered the concept of Treatment as Prevention (TasP®) and was the first to push for expanding HAART therapy to reduce both AIDS mortality and HIV transmission.

An Officer of the Order of Canada, Montaner has been inducted into the Canadian Medical Hall of Fame and awarded the Queen Elizabeth II Diamond Jubilee Medal for his research and advocacy. He remains a professor in the Faculty of Medicine and is the director of the British Columbia Centre for Excellence in HIV/AIDS.

One of the best-known examples of UBC's expertise in medical research arose out of another global health crisis. In 2002 a virus eventually known as severe acute respiratory syndrome (SARS) emerged from China's Guangdong province. Within three months, the virus was a global threat. Eight thousand people contracted it and 800 died.

Led by Marco Marra, a genetics professor at UBC, researchers in British Columbia were able to sequence the SARS genome in less than a week. This enabled Brett Finlay—a professor in the Michael Smith Laboratories, the Department of Biochemistry and Molecular Biology and the Department of Microbiology and Immunology at UBC—to form and lead the SARS Accelerated Vaccine Initiative (SAVI). Through SAVI, Finlay and his colleagues were able to develop three vaccine candidates within a year. Finlay is now a Distinguished Professor at UBC's Peter Wall Institute for Advanced Studies.

Collaboration has been the key to success in UBC's medical research. In 2015 two UBC researchers working out of the Vancouver Prostate Centre—run in partnership by UBC and the Vancouver Coastal Health Research Institute—developed a promising new treatment for drug-resistant prostate cancer.

above Students in the Faculty of Health and Social Development at UBC Okanagan.

Paul Rennie and Artem Cherkasov combined their talents in biology and innovative computer technology to design a new drug that targets mutated prostate cancer cells. The result was a treatment for a form of prostate cancer that previously was virtually incurable, and a $140-million licensing agreement with pharmaceutical manager Roche—the largest intellectual property fee in the university's history. The treatment has the potential to change the future of prostate cancer care.

Also on the forefront of global medical research is acclaimed geneticist Dr. Michael Hayden, professor in the Department of Medical Genetics and director of the Centre for Molecular Medicine and Therapeutics. The author of over 600 publications, Hayden is the most-cited author in the world on Huntington's disease, a hereditary and progressive brain disorder. Much of his work has focused on the genetic roots of Huntington's, and his findings have paved the way for developing effective prevention and treatment.

"When we started working on Huntington's disease, the future was dark and patients and families felt hopeless," said Hayden. "Today, that has all changed."

In 2017 Hayden was inducted into the Canadian Medical Hall of Fame and—along with Margaret Atwood, Roméo Dallaire, Leonard Cohen and David Suzuki—was listed in Ken McGoogan's book *50 Canadians Who Changed the World*.

Genetic research will continue to be a strong tradition at UBC, thanks to a major 2018 investment by the federal government. The Genome Canada Large-Scale Applied Research Project program contributed $101 million—nearly 40 per cent of the total national investment in genomics research—to projects led by the UBC Faculty of Medicine. Funded research includes developing a library of Indigenous genetic variation in Canada; creating a process for predicting the onset of childhood asthma; and uncovering biomarkers in patients that will show their probability of adverse drug reactions—starting with the most severe reactions that occur when treating children with cancer.

"What's exciting about these genomics and precision health projects is how clinically oriented they are," said Marc LePage, president and chief executive officer of Genome Canada. "Most are led by clinical scientists who deal with patients on a day-to-day basis and are well positioned to apply the research to healthcare settings ... they are not just about developing new therapies to treat diseases, but about early diagnosis and intervention to better curb or manage diseases at their onset."

facing The Vancouver Prostate Centre, which is a partnership between the university and the Vancouver Coastal Health Research Institute. The centre has developed a treatment for a form of prostate cancer that was previously virtually incurable.

above The Djavad Mowafaghian Centre for Brain Health helps to bridge the gap between research and clinical practice.

Djavad Mowafaghian Centre for Brain Health

One in three Canadians suffers from some form of brain disorder. Researchers at the Djavad Mowafaghian Centre for Brain Health continue to explore the causes, cures and treatments for a variety of conditions—including Alzheimer's, Parkinson's, Lou Gehrig's disease and multiple sclerosis.

Formerly known as the Brain Research Centre, the new 155,000-square-foot facility was opened in 2014. It builds on the existing partnership between Vancouver Coastal Health and UBC, helping to bridge the gap between research and clinical practice; putting expanded research in neuroscience, psychiatry and neurology under the same roof as advanced patient care.

above Dr. Peter Jepson-Young helped shift the conversation about HIV/AIDS in Canada.

ALUMNI
Dr. Peter Jepson-Young

Dr. Peter Jepson-Young graduated from UBC's Faculty of Science in 1979, and later returned to study medicine. After he earned his UBC medical degree, he was diagnosed with AIDS in 1986. At the time an essentially untreatable disease with myriad complications for immunity, it caused Jepson-Young to suffer pneumonia, two heart attacks and eventually a viral eye infection that left him blind.

Determined to fight the disease and to help others—particularly gay men such as himself who struggled with the stigma associated with homosexuality and AIDS—he worked with CBC Television to create a series called *Dr. Peter Diaries*. In 111 weekly episodes that aired over two years until his death in 1992, "Dr. Peter" spoke frankly about his experiences and helped shift public awareness of AIDS in Canada. A documentary about the series, *The Broadcast Tapes of Dr. Peter*, was nominated for an Oscar in 1994.

Before his death, Jepson-Young established the Dr. Peter AIDS Foundation, which grew to become the Dr. Peter Centre in Vancouver. Today the centre serves over 350 day health program participants and 50 residents annually. In 2016 the City of Vancouver honoured his memory by naming a lane in the West End after him.

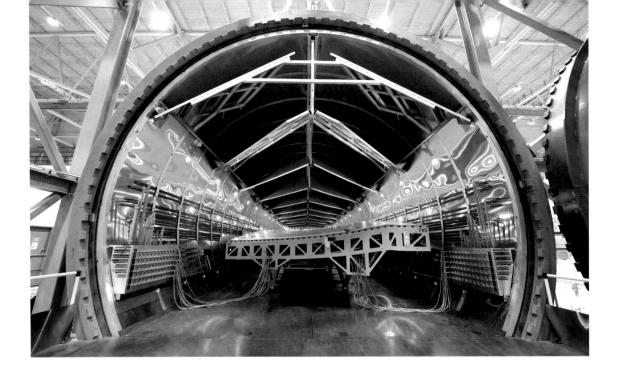

above UBC manufacturing science research underpinned the computer simulations used to design this autoclave, which Boeing uses to manufacture wings for the new 777X airplane.

Revolutionary Software

UBC materials engineering professor Anoush Poursartip is an expert in composite materials—high-strength, low-weight materials typically combining carbon fibre and plastic—used to make everything from golf clubs to jets.

To overcome the high costs of testing and building composite material prototypes, Poursartip's team developed software that lowers the risk of the process by simulating how an object is transformed as it is manufactured. This led to a partnership with Boeing that has, according to tech innovation publication *Research2Reality*, "revolutionized their composites manufacturing." Poursartip's work is allowing planes to fly farther and carry more weight while using less fuel.

Another UBC success story is AutoStitch, a software program that helps create striking, panoramic images from unordered collections of individual images. Developed by Matthew Brown in the early 2000s when he was a UBC computer science PhD candidate, the software uses algorithms to detect matches between images, and from there to form them into a seamless whole.

Brown's software has been commercialized for use in Windows and Apple systems and in film production—including a commercial licence to Lucasfilm's famed special-effects house, Industrial Light & Magic.

ALUMNI
Charlotte Froese Fischer

A pioneer in atomic structure theory and computer science, Charlotte Froese Fischer completed her UBC degree in mathematics and chemistry in 1952 and her Master of Arts in Applied Mathematics two years later. She returned to teach at UBC in 1957—the year the university got its first computer—after earning her PhD at Cambridge.

As a young UBC professor, Froese Fischer helped create the university's Computer Science Department. Her attempts to understand electron behaviour earned her the Alfred P. Sloan Foundation Research Fellowship, the first time it was awarded to a female scientist, and in 1991 she was made a Fellow of the American Physical Society.

The author of hundreds of research articles, Froese Fischer has been involved for over 25 years in the ITER project, the world's largest research effort focused on harnessing fusion energy, which brings together top scientists from 35 countries.

She is also a generous supporter of UBC, and has added gifts to the Department of Computer Science and the Institute of Applied Mathematics in her will. "UBC did a lot for me," Froese Fischer said. "I felt the support of the university, and I wanted to support someone else."

above Charlotte Froese Fischer, the first woman to receive the Alfred P. Sloan Foundation Research Fellowship, helped create UBC's Computer Science Department.

above The Centre for Social Innovation & Impact Investing (SauderS3i) assists businesses that tackle social and environmental challenges.

SauderS3i

Housed at the Sauder School of Business, the Centre for Social Innovation & Impact Investing (SauderS3i) is a UBC think-tank that researches and engages in business-based approaches to solving social and environmental challenges.

SauderS3i recruits students through a range of internships for graduate and postdoctoral fellows and acts as a champion of impact investing—supporting the investment of capital into businesses that generate environmental and social benefits along with monetary returns.

The "do well by doing good" field of impact investing continues to grow at an impressive rate thanks to pools of capital like the UBC

Social Impact Fund. Investments in the sector hit $228 billion in 2018, a more than fivefold increase since 2013.

To date, SauderS3i has put almost $5 million into Canada's impact investing ecosystem. The UBC Social Impact Fund, established by SauderS3i and managed by Innovation UBC, invests in ventures where at least one founder or key manager is a current UBC student, faculty, staff member or recent graduate.

Examples include Wize Monkey, a coffee leaf tea company that received the 2017 Small Business BC Award in the Best International Trade category, and ChopValue, which recycles used bamboo chopsticks into "a new building material which is carbon negative, durable and beautiful."

The centre also provides research support to the Impact Investment Forum, which assists individual investors, family offices and Canadian foundations in investing for a better world.

Survive and Thrive Applied Research

Wildfires are becoming more frequent in North America as a result of global warming. Raging fires present terrific dangers on the ground for communities, families and wildlife, and when they strike, another challenging situation plays out overhead for the aerial firefighting pilots who fly near to the blazes to contain them with water and fire retardant.

One company providing aerial firefighting services is Conair, based in Abbotsford, BC. When Transport Canada proposed new rules governing pilot fatigue, Conair wanted to conduct research to see if the guidelines were actually appropriate for their pilots.

To do so, they approached UBC Okanagan's Survive and Thrive Applied Research (STAR) program, which joins civil society partners with university researchers in solving human survival and performance challenges. Describing itself as "a research, development and demonstration (R&D&D) initiative that develops technology products, standards and strategies," STAR offers access to leading-edge data as well as 3-D scanning, rapid prototyping and an off-campus blast and ballistics lab.

To assist Conair, STAR connected with UBC Okanagan research teams in a variety of disciplines—including the School of Engineering; the Department of Computer Science, Mathematics, Physics and Statistics; and the School of Health and Exercise Sciences. Partners from Camosun College and Latitude Technologies, a flight data company based in Victoria, also assisted with the research.

This dream team of talented researchers worked to better understand the way that fatigue affects pilots' ability to fly, and to develop an automated pilot fatigue risk management system for aerial firebombers.

STAR researchers have assisted in several other projects, including exploring the design of new helmets to ensure the safety of participants in concussion-inducing sports, and designing oxygen-sensing masks for endurance athletes.

NanoMat

Small things can make big changes. Despite being less than 1/1000th the width of a human hair, nanomaterials are having major impacts globally on computing technology, healthcare, alternative energy and environmental restoration.

Like many other countries, Canada has a growing demand for highly qualified nanomaterial trainees. In response, in 2014 UBC chemist Mark MacLachlan—with funding from the Natural Sciences and Engineering Research Council of Canada—launched the Collaborative Research and Training Experience Program in Nanomaterials Science and Technology (NanoMat).

The Faculty of Science interdisciplinary program allows science and engineering graduate students, as well as postdoctoral fellows, to develop their skills in hands-on nanomaterials research. NanoMat trainees can focus their collaborative research projects in one of three areas: alternative energy, the environment or health.

Students are also given courses in leadership and communication skills and are required to complete internships at national and international companies—giving them the opportunity to become leaders in building a better world with this emergent technology.

facing UBC Okanagan's Survive and Thrive Applied Research (STAR) program brings civil society partners together with university researchers to solve human survival and performance challenges.

Centre for the Study of Democratic Institutions

The Centre for the Study of Democratic Institutions (CSDI) brings together scholars, public officials and students to generate new ideas for strengthening democracy in Canada and beyond.

It's timely work relevant around the world, as the centre notes when describing its mission: "The benefits of democracy and good governance are increasingly at risk, as once-exemplary democracies lose their attractiveness, and vulnerable democracies are drifting into the gray zone between electoral democracy and authoritarianism. Perhaps even more troubling is the array of global challenges democracies now face, including threats to financial stability, energy supply, public health, and the global climate."

Headed by Maxwell Cameron, a noted scholar of Latin American politics, CSDI has convened international workshops on human

development and the quality of democracy, Indigenous rights and self-determination, and more. Closer to home, CSDI staged a round-table event to educate British Columbians during the 2018 lead-up to the province's referendum on proportional representation.

The centre also offers the annual Summer Institute for Future Legislators, an innovative course for aspiring politicians. Via experiential learning and coaching—both from political veterans and scholars of Canadian democracy—participants cultivate the skills they will need to work effectively as elected legislators.

Mentoring has been provided by former Vancouver mayor (and now senator) Larry Campbell, former deputy prime minister Anne McLellan, past BC premier Mike Harcourt, former BC finance minister Joy MacPhail and many others.

facing and above
Students debating at the Summer Institute for Future Legislators.

Population and Public Health

UBC's School of Population and Public Health (SPPH) trains students to shape and improve healthcare systems in Canada and around the world.

Student and faculty researchers at the school—nested within the Faculty of Medicine—contribute to global health through hands-on experience and analyses. They have advocated for harm-reduction approaches to the opioid overdose crisis and researched the deadly impacts of air pollution in urban areas. During the 2014 Ebola outbreak, the SPPH community offered advice on designing clinical trials, assisted the World Health Organization in creating infection control plans, and helped develop preparedness plans for British Columbia.

The Centre for Excellence in Indigenous Health, established by SPPH in 2014, was created to foster and support Indigenous health programs locally and around the world. It provides a way for Indigenous communities to connect directly with UBC's programs and health researchers, and provides a one-stop location for training and resources related to Indigenous health.

The centre is currently working with the BC First Nations Health Authority and other partners to increase the number of Indigenous students becoming health professionals and to raise awareness of the health challenges facing Indigenous peoples in Canada.

Other ongoing efforts and initiatives include, among many others, studying how urban design can lead to better health outcomes;

examining the impacts of prescription drug pricing; and research by SPPH professor Joel Singer (part of a Bill and Melinda Gates Foundation–funded initiative) on reducing pre-eclampsia deaths among women in Pakistan, India, Nigeria and Mozambique.

above HATCH is an incubator for tech start-ups, whose biggest success story so far is Acuva, a manufacturer of UV-based water-purification devices.

HATCH: Fostering Entrepreneurship

An incubator for tech start-up companies, HATCH is where aspiring UBC entrepreneurs go to move fresh ideas from the laboratory to the marketplace.

HATCH works with selected researchers and entrepreneurs who have already validated a business idea, providing mentorship along with project and meeting space. Before coming to HATCH, many researchers benefit from UBC's Small Business Accelerator, which provides free tools for due-diligence market research.

Perhaps the incubator's biggest success story to date is Acuva, a company that designs and manufactures energy-efficient water-purification devices that use ultraviolet light to clear drinking water of pathogens.

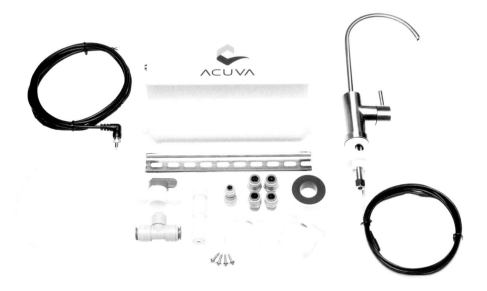

above Acuva's energy-efficient, low-maintenance design could help the device save lives in developing countries.

Acuva was born in 2014 after UBC MBA grad Manoj Singh paired up with UBC chemical and biological engineering professor Fariborz Taghipour, the original developer of the technology. Singh saw commercial potential—and the possibility to do social good—immediately.

Unlike most ultraviolet-light methods of disinfection, Taghipour's technology is energy-efficient and low-maintenance. It is currently being marketed toward North American cottagers and RV owners, but Singh's vision is to eventually bring the device to developing countries like India, where it could potentially save lives.

"We're not just a water-purification company," said Singh. "We're a UBC-inspired technology company that knows how to kill pathogens. We'll continue to partner with UBC to develop new markets for this technology to clean water, air and even medical devices."

Stewart Blusson Quantum Matter Institute and TRIUMF/Isotope Separator and Accelerator

Originally founded as the Quantum Matter Institute in 2010 and rededicated as the Stewart Blusson Quantum Matter Institute (SBQMI) in 2016, the SBQMI has a mission to "discover, design and build the quantum technologies of the future." To do that requires deeper understanding of the nature and phenomena of quantum materials—and that takes research.

Quantum matter research analyzes the behaviour of particles at the atomic level—where nature leaves the laws of Newtonian physics behind—and the opportunities these sometimes unusual behaviours present for new technologies like topological insulators and superconductors. Discoveries related to quantum materials are predicted to revolutionize electronics, medicine and sustainable energy production.

above Home to UBC's Isotope Separator and Accelerator, the ISAC-II facility also houses research and office space for the TRIUMF particle accelerator project.

top TRIUMF began in 1968 as a joint venture project between UBC, SFU and the University of Victoria.

bottom Justin Trudeau visiting TRIUMF in 2018.

The SBQMI builds on a tradition of cutting-edge subatomic physics research at UBC, established in part by TRIUMF, Canada's particle accelerator centre. The lab, which began in 1968 as a joint project between UBC, Simon Fraser University and the University of Victoria, has grown to include 20 member universities and now provides research space for over 600 scientists, engineers and staff on its sprawling south campus site of nearly 13 acres.

Each year, TRIUMF hosts hundreds of users from around the world and provides research opportunities in a wide range of topics—including particle and nuclear physics, materials sciences and life sciences—to over 100 students and postdoctoral fellows.

TRIUMF's Isotope Separator and Accelerator facility, which came online in 1999, is a multidisciplinary isotope research centre that continues to perform important research in materials science, astrophysics and radiochemistry, as well as in subatomic and nuclear physics.

above In 2018, TRIUMF researchers and staff gathered to welcome Governor General Julie Payette to the facility.

The Spirit of Competition

above and facing
UBC's collegiate athletic program is the most decorated in the country. To date, more than 220 UBC students and graduates have represented Canada at the Olympics, winning over 65 medals.

A Winning Tradition

Students from UBC have been making their contribution to the sporting world since the university sent its first athlete to the Olympics in 1928. To date, more than 220 UBC students and graduates have represented Canada at the Olympics, winning over 65 medals for the country.

The university's collegiate athletics program—which includes the UBC Thunderbirds and the UBC Okanagan Heat—encompasses 25 varsity teams across 14 sports and is the most successful and decorated in the country.

As of 2018, UBC held 149 national and 219 regional championship titles. Some of UBC's most awarded programs are men's and women's swimming, soccer and basketball; women's volleyball, golf and field hockey; and men's football.

UBC's varsity swimming history is almost as old as the university itself, and is arguably one of the Thunderbirds' strongest athletic traditions. UBC has won 22 national women's championships and 16 national men's championships, along with many more regional titles.

During UBC's "Decade of Dominance" from 1998 to 2007, both the men's and women's swim teams won 10 consecutive national championships. Both teams are once again sweeping regional championships, and—since the opening of UBC's new Aquatic Centre in 2017—national competitions as well.

Men's and women's varsity golf is another strong tradition at UBC. In the 15 years leading up to 2018, the Thunderbirds won the women's national championship every year but three. The relatively new golf teams from UBC Okanagan, meanwhile, have been leaders in their

own right, with the Heat women's team capturing national silver in 2015 and national bronze in 2018, and the men's team winning national silver in 2017.

ALUMNI

Kathleen Heddle

Kathleen Heddle's first choice in sports was volleyball. But in her third year at UBC she saw a booth for the rowing team while she was registering for courses at War Memorial Gym. Intrigued, she signed up, and after just one year on the team was considered one of the university's best rowers, drawing the attention of Olympic coaches.

"I was hooked right away," said Heddle. "I liked the balance between brute strength and power with finesse."

The next year, Heddle won gold at the 1987 Pan American Games. Heddle graduated from UBC with a degree in psychology in 1990, and went on to compete in two Olympic Games—winning two golds in Barcelona in 1992 for the women's coxed eight and women's coxless pair, and gold and bronze medals in Atlanta in 1996 for women's double and quad sculls, respectively.

Her wins have made her and her rowing partner, Marnie McBean, the only Canadian athletes to receive three gold medals in the Summer Olympic Games. Heddle has also won three gold medals and one silver medal in the World Rowing Championships.

facing top UBC's golf teams are frequent winners of national championship medals.

facing bottom Kathleen Heddle's rowing career placed her in the pantheon of great Canadian athletes.

above Members of the Thunderbirds rowing team stretching out.

facing The Duke and Duchess of Cambridge visiting UBC Okanagan in 2016.

Following her retirement from competitive rowing in 1996, Heddle received the rowing world's highest honour—the International Rowing Federation's Thomas Keller Medal, given in recognition of her sportsmanship and record-setting career.

She is a member of the Order of British Columbia (1997) and a hall of famer for the Canadian Olympics (1994), Canada Sports (1997), UBC Sports (2002) and British Columbia Sports (2003).

Heddle has worked with the International Rowing Federation, including as chair of the Athletes Commission, and remains active in sports administration.

The Duke and Duchess of Cambridge at UBC Okanagan

In 2016, celebrations of the 10th anniversary of the UBC Okanagan campus received some royal attention with the visit of the Duke and Duchess of Cambridge. The next generation of English royalty stopped by UBC on their countrywide tour of Canada, dedicating a new Indigenous art installation and watching an exhibition match of the UBC Okanagan Heat women's volleyball team—an excellent choice, as in 2018 the team was ranked first in Canada by coaches across the country.

above Storm the Wall is a four-part endurance race that culminates in climbing a 3.7-metre wall.

Storm the Wall

Students at UBC have long been fond of outdoor recreation, and sometimes adding a little competition makes it even more fun. Storm the Wall is a tradition at the Vancouver campus that has been going strong since 1978. Relay teams (or solo "Iron Legends") attempt to cap a four-part endurance race—including swimming, sprinting, cycling and a 1.5-kilometre run—by climbing a 3.7-metre wall. Storm the Wall has become the largest intramural sporting event in North America, with over 4,000 participants each year.

Doug Mitchell Thunderbird Sports Centre

With three ice arenas for Thunderbirds hockey, events and lessons, the Doug Mitchell Thunderbird Sports Centre is a hockey and skating hub for the university and the greater community. The stadium

arena can hold up to 7,000 people for Thunderbirds games, concerts and other events, and the ice can be expanded to the size needed for Olympic competition.

The other two ice surfaces—Father David Bauer Arena and Protrans Arena—are mainly used for training, learn-to-skate programs and non-Thunderbirds ice hockey.

Nearby is the Vancouver Whitecaps FC National Soccer Development Centre, a training facility with dressing rooms, meeting space and a 4,100-square-foot training area.

above No longer a mud bowl, Thunderbird Stadium can seat up to 3,500 fans for football games and rugby matches.

Thunderbird Stadium

Built in 1967 to replace aging Varsity Stadium, Thunderbird Stadium is where up to 3,500 fans can gather to watch football and rugby teams battle it out on the field. Once known as the "mud bowl" for the

above UBC graduate Andrea Neil, a pioneer of Canadian women's soccer, is one of the country's most renowned players.

effects of Vancouver rains during fall and winter games, the playing field is now covered in high-performance, stadium-grade artificial turf—the first in British Columbia to receive two-star certification from FIFA.

ALUMNI
Andrea Neil

Before becoming one of Canada's most renowned soccer players, Vancouver native Andrea Neil was UBC's top female athlete in 1993, and she led the Thunderbirds to a national championship in 1994.

A pioneer of Canadian women's soccer, the human kinetics graduate went on to play with the Canadian national team for 17 years, including at four FIFA Women's World Cups. She represented her country in international competitions 132 times—which at the time of her retirement in 2007 was more than any Canadian player in history.

She simultaneously built a record-setting career with Vancouver's pro soccer team, the Whitecaps, which she took to two championships as team captain and assistant coach. She has been honoured with multiple sports hall of fame inductions from UBC, British Columbia and Canada.

Aquatic Centre

At the London Summer Olympics in 2012, more Canadian competitive swimmers were from UBC than anywhere else in the country. The Thunderbirds swim team is truly world-class, and their need for up-to-date training facilities was one of the motives for building the Aquatic Centre. But it wasn't the only one: UBC also wanted to ensure that the rest of its students—as well as residents in nearby neighbourhoods—had the chance to use modern, accessible swimming facilities.

This left UBC, and architects Acton Ostry, with some big questions: "Can the centre train Olympic-quality athletes, serve the larger community and provide a place that will enrich the experience of our students? And is it possible to build a facility where you're teaching kids to swim while running an international meet with hundreds of competitors?"

The answer to both questions was yes. When the $39-million Aquatic Centre opened in 2017, it proved that it was able to serve as

above and overleaf
Built to LEED Gold standards of environmental design, the Aquatic Centre features a 25-metre recreational pool, a 50-metre competition pool and a children's pool, among other amenities.

above The $39-million Aquatic Centre opened in 2017.

both a competition/training venue and a community aquatic centre—able to meet the needs of nationally ranked athletes while also offering a place where students, families and neighbourhood residents can enjoy swimming for exercise and recreation.

The centre features a 25-metre recreational pool, a 50-metre competition pool and a children's pool complete with a "lazy river." It can accommodate 1,000 swimmers and waders, and up to 460 spectators.

Built to target LEED Gold standards of environmental design, the Aquatic Centre incorporates recycled and locally sourced materials as well as sustainably harvested wood. Fittingly for a swimming centre, it was also created as a water-saving demonstration project. Rain-water collected in a massive underground water cistern is used in the pools after being cleaned with diatomaceous earth, chlorine and ultraviolet light—saving about 2.7 million litres annually.

In 2018 the Aquatic Centre was awarded a Global Architecture and Design Award in the Sports and Recreation category.

Day of the LongBoat

A UBC tradition since 1987, the Day of the LongBoat gathers more than 3,000 participants to Jericho Beach for a day of spirited paddling. The world's largest voyageur canoe race brings out teams of UBC students, faculty and staff, graduates and community members to navigate an ocean racecourse—rain or shine.

Some canoe just for fun, while others race in competitive heats. LongBoat winners walk away with the prestigious Day of the Long-Boat trophy, a UBC intramurals champion shirt and, of course, a little swagger.

A day of camaraderie, competition and capsizes for participants, the Day of the LongBoat festival on the beach is also a magnet for spectators. A free shuttle bus carries students from campus to Jericho Beach, where UBC Recreation runs beach games and an emcee gives the blow-by-blow of the races.

Extraordinary Collections

above Koerner Library, seen here at sunset, houses over a million volumes.

UBC Library

These days, checking out a book from one of UBC Library's 20 branches is a simple matter for students, faculty and community members. But when the university first set out to obtain books for the library in 1915, administrators experienced a much greater challenge—and accusations of espionage.

In 1914 J.T. Gerould, a librarian from the University of Minnesota, was hired to travel to Europe to purchase a starting collection of books for UBC's imminent library. World War I broke out while Gerould was in Germany, and he was detained in Leipzig for three weeks under suspicion of being a British spy. The evidence against him was a mysterious document German officials found in his luggage—a copy of the proposed UBC site plan. Fortunately, before being detained, Gerould was able to purchase and ship 20,000 volumes, enough for the beginning of a basic university library collection.

Over the last century, UBC Library has grown to become one of Canada's top academic research libraries, containing 5.5 million books, journals, maps, musical scores and audiovisual materials—as well as more than 2 million e-books.

Branches and divisions on the Vancouver campus include the Walter C. Koerner Library, which houses almost a million volumes and a generous amount of study space, and the Irving K. Barber Learning Centre, which contains the majority of UBC Library's special collections. The library also maintains branches on the UBC Okanagan campus and one at Vancouver General Hospital.

Outside the library walls, administrators and staff ensure the institution is an active part of the UBC community as well, hosting unique exhibits and events, engaging with the Musqueam community and participating in UBC's Pride Picnic.

above The Irving K. Barber Learning Centre contains the majority of UBC Library's special collections.

EXTRAORDINARY COLLECTIONS

153

above "The Belkin" is a rich archive of Vancouver's art history, particularly of avant-garde works of the 1960s and 1970s.

Morris and Helen Belkin Art Gallery

Founded in 1948 as the UBC Fine Arts Gallery, the Morris and Helen Belkin Art Gallery was rededicated under its present name in 1995—after being moved to a striking new space designed by Vancouver architect Peter Cardew. In its location on Main Mall, it continues to do what originally put it on the map: highlight innovative artists and explore new boundaries of contemporary art.

"The Belkin" is home to close to 5,000 works and is one of the largest public art collections in British Columbia. It is also a rich archive of Vancouver's art history in the post-war period, particularly of avant-garde works of the 1960s and 1970s.

In recent years, artists Lawrence Paul Yuxweluptun, Judy Radul and Jack Shadbolt have all been highlighted in solo exhibitions.

Recent displays have focused on the perspectives and creations of Indigenous artists, such as Beau Dick, Dana Claxton, Marianne Nicolson, and Jeneen Frei Njootli and other members of the ReMatriate Collective.

The Belkin mounts four major exhibitions each year, but is much more than a display space. The gallery also curates smaller travelling exhibitions and hosts concerts, symposia and events—as well as loaning work from its collection for international exhibitions.

Outdoor art continues to be an important and unique aspect of UBC's art collection. The Belkin has been collecting works of outdoor art to enrich the campus environment and prominently showcase diverse voices. Many of them—like Esther Shalev-Gerz's *The Shadow* and Edgar Heap of Birds' *Native Hosts* installation of aluminum signs—prompt viewers to think about the ecological and cultural realities that are inseparable from daily life at UBC.

Museum of Anthropology

When the Museum of Anthropology (MOA) building was designed by architect Arthur Erickson in the mid-1970s, he took inspiration from the cedar post-and-beam dwellings built by the Indigenous peoples of the northwest coast—and envisioned the building as "a work of light and shadows... designed to resonate to the metronome of the seasons and the diverse cultural collections which it houses."

above The Museum of Anthropology is a magnificent space conserving 50,000 objects from around the world.

above Museum of Anthropology architect Arthur Erickson envisioned the building as "a work of light and shadows" that would artfully house its diverse cultural displays and adapt to the shifting seasons.

It's a magnificent space filled with numinous things. MOA houses about 50,000 objects from around the world, from a 15th-century Inca quipu abacus to yokes for rice-paddy cattle used by the Hakka people of China.

Pieces by contemporary Musqueam artists Susan Point and Joe Becker greet you as you enter the building, and once inside, you're treated to the works of Haida artist Bill Reid. Perhaps the most spectacular sculpture in the museum is Reid's *The Raven and the First Men*. Carved from a four-tonne block of laminated yellow cedar, the work depicts the Raven coaxing the first Haida to emerge from a clamshell. Architect Erickson specially designed the museum's rotunda to house the colossal sculpture, which had to be lowered into place with a crane.

A 2010 expansion boosted MOA's facilities by 50 per cent, adding new research spaces as well as the Audrey and Harry Hawthorn Library and Archives, which offers an oral history and language lab.

above UBC Library's Videomatica Collection of over 35,000 titles includes rare and historic films along with feature, cult, foreign and art films.

MOA now has one of the most advanced and comprehensive research infrastructures of any museum in North America.

An online catalogue provides access to over 45,000 objects, and web technology continues to shape the museum's engagement with Indigenous peoples. The Reciprocal Research Network is an online tool to facilitate reciprocal and collaborative research about cultural heritage, developed by MOA in partnership with the Musqueam, the Stó:lō Nation and the U'mista Cultural Society. The Reciprocal Research Network makes objects from MOA and 27 other institutions accessible online to enable communities, cultural institutions and researchers to work together. As of 2019, the MOA items catalogued there have been viewed more than 10 million times.

MOA also supports the Indigitization Program, which assists in the conservation, digitization and management of Indigenous community knowledge.

Videomatica, Uno Langmann Family and H. Colin Slim Stravinsky Collections

UBC Library supports teaching and learning at UBC as a repository for the latest research and data, and it's also a portal offering access to archival resources and unusual collections. Sometimes these collections are remote, only accessible via the library's online Open Collections site; and sometimes they're right in the building with you.

When Videomatica—one of Vancouver's most legendary independent DVD rental locations, famous for stocking offbeat films—faced the fate that eventually befell bigger movie-rental chains like Blockbuster, UBC and SFU stepped in to save its uniquely curated library.

Videomatica co-founders Graham Peat and Brian Bosworth are both former UBC students, and when Vancouver philanthropist Yosef Wosk heard they were shutting their doors, he facilitated a donation and purchase agreement to have UBC preserve the collection.

The collection of over 35,000 titles includes rare and historic films; feature, cult and art films; foreign films from more than 75 countries; and an assortment of Canadian works that includes many selections from the Vancouver International Film Festival. Most of them are now available through UBC Library's Koerner branch, and the library continues to add to the collection.

The university's Videomatica collection is one of several special holdings at UBC Library. Another is the Uno Langmann Family Collection of photographs chronicling BC history from the 1850s to the 1970s.

Donated by Uno and Dianne Langmann, the 18,000 photos span a wide range of demographics and geography, from young German women in the gold rush town of Barkerville to Indigenous Elders on northern Vancouver Island.

While considerably smaller in size than the Langmann photo archive, the H. Colin Slim Stravinsky Collection is one of UBC Library's most prized possessions for classical music enthusiasts: more than 130 letters, scores and memorabilia documenting the work and life of composer Igor Stravinsky.

The first question that comes to mind for many is: What is Stravinsky's connection to UBC?

While a student in UBC's School of Music in 1952, H. Colin Slim participated in two premiere performances of Stravinsky's *Les Noces (Cantata in Four Scenes)*—which Slim conducted—and *Concerto for Two Pianos*. Six months later, Slim spent time driving with the composer to rehearsals when Stravinsky came to Vancouver to guest-direct the Vancouver Symphony Orchestra. Fourteen years after that, Slim and Stravinsky met once again, this time backstage in Los Angeles after Slim performed in two choral pieces directed by Stravinsky.

These encounters clearly made an impact on Slim. He went on to become a prominent musicologist and orchestral conductor, and he began collecting artifacts documenting Stravinsky's life and

facing Igor Stravinsky, seen here conducting, was a source of fascination to H. Colin Slim, who donated his collection of Stravinsky artifacts to UBC Library.

facing *facing* Scale model
of the *Empress of
Asia* ocean liner on
display with the Chung
Collection.

work—including, as UBC Library notes, "a signed edition of his bal-
let *Petrushka*, an inscribed book of his *Poetics of Music,* and numerous
autographed items." Slim donated his extensive collection to UBC in
1999 and has continued to add to it over the years.

Wallace B. Chung and Madeline H. Chung Collection

Born in Victoria in 1925, Wallace Bakfu Chung was only six years
old when he began collecting newspaper and magazine clippings.
Inspired by his grandfather's emigration voyage from China to Victoria in the early 1900s—and intrigued by a poster of the ocean liner
RMS *Empress of Asia* that hung in his father's tailor shop—Chung
began what would become a 60-year passion for documenting early
BC history and North American immigration.

In 1953 Dr. Wallace Chung married Dr. Madeline Huang. They were
pioneers in their own right, being two of the first Chinese Canadians
to pursue medical careers. Wallace became a vascular surgeon and
ultimately head of the Department of Surgery at UBC Hospital, retiring in 1991. Madeline specialized in obstetrics and gynecology and
delivered over 7,000 babies during her long career, including many
of the Chinese Canadian children born in the Greater Vancouver area.

While attending to his own career and raising a family, Chung
steadily grew his collection to what it is today: more than 25,000

unique artifacts that provide a window into the experience of early Chinese Canadians, as well as the history of the Canadian Pacific Railway. His trove of documents, books, maps, paintings, photographs and other items is one of the most exceptional and extensive collections of its kind in North America.

In 1999 the Chungs gifted their extensive collection to UBC Library's Irving K. Barber Learning Centre. Housed in the Rare Books and Special Collections section, the exhibit is open to the public, and admission is free. Chung has stated his hope that his gift will ensure "as many people as possible can have the opportunity to understand and appreciate the struggles and joys of those who have come before them."

The Chung Collection was recently made accessible to an even wider audience online. Thousands of items are available for viewing on the UBC Library website, with new content added regularly. A 2014 documentary film produced by UBC Library, titled *Passage of Dreams: The Chung Collection*, features personal stories by Chung about the collection and Chinese Canadian history.

Fostering Sustainability

A Living Lab

A "sandbox for sustainability" may not be the first thing that comes to mind when you think of UBC's Vancouver campus, but that's one way to describe it: an independently run, 990-acre miniature of the global built environment, where students, faculty and university partners can create and test innovative new forms.

The university's Vancouver campus hosts 56,000 students and 15,000 faculty and staff—a small city, with all the physical plant capacities that such a place requires. UBC owns and operates all the facilities for its more than 500 buildings, including electrical, heating, water and waste utilities. The university even maintains its own roads and other external infrastructure.

That could be a burden, but it's also an opportunity. It makes the campus into a living lab for exploring and testing out new environmental, social, economic and technological advances, some of which could be scaled up to move the needle on global sustainability. As a result of these and other efforts, in 2019 Times Higher Education ranked UBC as the number-one university in the world for taking action to fight climate change and its impacts—and first in Canada for helping cities become safe, inclusive, resilient and sustainable.

One example of UBC's sustainability innovations is the new Academic District Energy System (ADES), which replaced—piece by piece, over seven years from 2011 to 2018—14 kilometres of steam piping that had been in use for 90 years. District energy is an innovative and

increasingly common form of integrated heating that works well for clusters of buildings in urban areas and universities. The result of the switch to ADES is an efficient hot water heating system that serves 160 buildings and has cut energy consumption by 24 per cent.

In 2012 the university unveiled its Bioenergy Research Demonstration Facility (BRDF), a $27.4-million energy-generation facility created with partners Nexterra Systems and GE. BRDF transforms two to three truckloads of ground and chipped waste wood daily into heat and electricity for use on campus.

Another example of the "living lab" approach to innovation is the Energy Storage System, a $5-million project that will use lithium-ion batteries to regulate the energy to the BRDF as a first step in a broader, campus-wide smart grid project.

As UBC Sustainability put it: "As owner-operators, we have discretion to try new things. As researchers, we have an incentive to try new things first. This is the essence of the campus as a living laboratory."

Centre for Interactive Research on Sustainability

The mission of the Centre for Interactive Research on Sustainability (CIRS) is to foster better, more sustainable building practices and green urban development. The CIRS Building itself was, therefore, held to an understandably high standard.

facing The CIRS Building incorporates living green walls and roofs, as well as systems that harvest, clean and reuse rainwater.

Inspired by founder John Robinson's concept of "restorative sustainability"—the idea that the built environment can actually improve our surroundings rather than degrade them—CIRS models ways to use construction resources more efficiently.

The four-storey building was designed by Busby Perkins + Will architects. It incorporates living green walls and roofs, systems that harvest, clean and reuse rainwater, and a geoexchange system that keeps it warm in winter and cool in summer.

Completed in 2011, it was the first UBC building to achieve the LEED Platinum standard and it continues to function as a testing ground for innovative approaches to architecture and urban design.

ALUMNI

Mathabo Tsepa

Mathabo Tsepa is a diplomat and human rights advocate who has devoted herself to improving life for the people of her native Lesotho—particularly in the areas of food security, access to clean water and sanitation.

Tsepa earned her PhD in environmental education from UBC in 2008, after which she returned to Lesotho, where she served as high commissioner to Canada from 2010 to 2016. She would later serve in multiple diplomatic postings, including ambassador of Lesotho to Cuba.

In collaboration with UBC's Go Global initiative, Tsepa has helped to send UBC students to her home district of Qacha's Nek in southern Lesotho. Students have assisted in creating a preschool for orphans and in building latrines that significantly decrease waterborne disease.

Tsepa continues to share ideas and research on place management via a cultural exchange program between UBC and the National University of Lesotho.

Marine Conservation

UBC's Vancouver campus overlooks the Pacific Ocean, and nearby beaches are favourite destinations for student recreation. But coastal marine ecosystems mean more to the UBC community than just beautiful views or places to play volleyball.

At the Institute for the Oceans and Fisheries (IOF)—founded in 1950—global and local experts across many disciplines work to better understand coastal ecosystems and the communities that rely on them. The institute's Aboriginal Fisheries Research Unit combines

above A female Patagonian seahorse (*Hippocampus patagonicus*).

traditional ecological knowledge and modern analyses to ensure sustainable fisheries for Indigenous peoples.

Researchers with the Changing Ocean Research Unit, meanwhile, are examining the impacts of global warming on people as well as ocean species, and exploring ways to adapt to and mitigate them.

Another IOF initiative is Project Seahorse, which was co-founded in 1996 by the institute's Amanda Vincent in partnership with the Zoological Society of London. The award-winning international conservation group uses seahorses as a flagship indicator species to advocate for healthy, well-managed marine ecosystems.

Project Seahorse has established 35 "no-take" marine protected areas in the Philippines and created a regional coalition of 1,000 low-income Filipino fishing families who are helping protect seahorses and shallow-water habitats.

The initiative has also engaged with multiple interest groups to move traditional Chinese medicine toward sustainable practices, and—under the Convention on International Trade in Endangered Species (CITES)—helped catalyze the first global export controls for marine fish of commercial importance. Along the way, they have trained over 175 conservationists and many more citizen scientists.

The IOF's Marine Mammal Research Unit studies animals in the North Pacific—particularly Steller sea lions, harbour seals, northern fur seals and orca. Part of its focus on marine mammal conservation includes reducing conflicts in the ocean between marine mammals and human uses. The research unit also runs UBC's Open Water Research Station in Port Moody, the world's only open-ocean lab with free-swimming, trained sea lions assisting with diving and foraging research.

In 2017 the Tula Foundation joined forces with UBC Science to create the Hakai Coastal Initiative. Intended to advance the state of research on the coast, the initiative brings together postdoctoral fellows and graduate students with established researchers. It includes seven working groups on a variety of subject areas, including salmon, shellfish, marine food webs, nearshore ecology and ocean modelling.

above The Hakai Coastal Initiative (HCI) studies food webs and nearshore ecology in BC's kelp forests, along with other areas of oceanography and marine biodiversity. HCI is one of many research collaborations at UBC's Institute for the Oceans and Fisheries.

above, right and facing The Bamfield Marine Sciences Centre provides world-class research infrastructure for marine scientists.

UBC undergraduates and IOF graduate students can apply to do research at the stunning Bamfield Marine Sciences Centre (BMSC), a campus shared with several other universities that has a mandate to provide "world-class research infrastructure" for marine scientists. The Bamfield centre offers students and faculty access to the incredible marine diversity of Vancouver Island's western coast and over 32,000 square feet of laboratory space.

above Visitors to the Greenheart TreeWalk get a rare chance to experience the canopy of a temperate rainforest.

Up in the Air

The Greenheart TreeWalk at the UBC Botanical Garden is a 310-metre aerial trail system hung from giant Douglas fir, grand fir and cedar trees. Visitors can wander its walkways or join a naturalist-led tour of the flora and fauna of a rarely visited ecosystem: the canopy of a coastal temperate rainforest.

A collaboration between UBC Botanical Garden and Greenheart—a Vancouver-based company that specializes in creating aerial trails—the TreeWalk was opened in 2008 and welcomes over 13,000 visitors a year.

Tallwood House

Built in 2017, Tallwood House provides beds for over 400 UBC students. The structure is unique: at 18 storeys, it's the tallest "mass timber" building in the world.

Mass timber buildings are built to have a reduced reliance on concrete, which can generate higher carbon emissions than wood. The innovative structure—which no doubt pleased the Faculty of Forestry—incorporates 1.7 million board feet of lumber, with cross-laminated timber floors and walls and load-bearing glulam timbers, as well as concrete.

Building Tallwood House in this way is estimated to have saved 2,400 tonnes of carbon dioxide compared with traditional methods—about the same as taking 400 cars off the road for a year.

FOSTERING SUSTAINABILITY

above David Suzuki's academic career spanned more than 30 years as a professor in UBC's Department of Zoology—where, along with his many other achievements, he inspired the creation of an iconic pub.

David Suzuki: An Environmental Icon

Scientist, environmental activist and Canadian media icon David Suzuki is the author and co-author of more than 50 books. He is best known for bringing science to the mainstream through his CBC Television show *The Nature of Things*—which he began hosting in 1979—and for the environmental foundation that bears his name.

Born in Vancouver in 1936, Suzuki was six years old when he and his family were forced into a Japanese internment camp in the BC Interior during World War II. Despite that difficult experience, he excelled in his studies and after the war went on to earn his undergraduate biology degree from Amherst College in Massachusetts and his PhD in zoology from the University of Chicago. Before retiring in 2001, his career at UBC spanned more than 30 years as a professor in the Department of Zoology—where in addition to his many academic achievements, he's credited with inspiring the creation of the now-iconic UBC pub called the Pit.

He founded the not-for-profit David Suzuki Foundation in 1990, placing him at the forefront of battles over clear-cut logging, salmon farming, climate change and many other issues.

Suzuki has won five Gemini Awards for his broadcasting, received 29 honorary degrees from around the English-speaking world and been named to the Order of Canada. In 2000 UBC presented him with an award for lifetime achievement.

Beaty Biodiversity Museum

Known for its very visible, 26-metre, reassembled skeleton of a blue whale—one of just 21 on display in the world—the Beaty Biodiversity Museum is Vancouver's only natural history museum.

The museum plays a crucial role in the educational environs of UBC as a space dedicated to helping students, faculty and the general public value their relationship with the natural world, and inspiring them to protect it.

Opened in 2010, the museum is part of UBC's Biodiversity Research Centre. More than 50 renowned biodiversity researchers work at the centre, studying the factors and forces that sustain life on the planet, as well as the forces that lead to habitat loss and species extinction—from genetics to ecosystems to human society.

The Beaty Biodiversity Museum contains 500 exhibits and 2 million specimens for visitors to explore, some of which are potent

above The 500 displays at the Beaty Biodiversity Museum remind visitors of the beauty and fragility of life on Earth.

reminders of the fragility of life on Earth. Displays include three sets of dinosaur track casts from British Columbia's early Cretaceous period, a rare red panda skull, and samples of extinct species such as the passenger pigeon, along with fossils, reptiles, insects and plants from Canada and around the world.

UBC Farm and the Centre for Sustainable Food Systems

Located on the southern edge of the Vancouver campus, UBC Farm is a celebrated food hub and outdoor classroom run by the Centre for Sustainable Food Systems (CSFS). The farm encompasses nearly 60 acres of orchards, annual crop fields, pasture and teaching gardens.

As factors like population growth, climate change and urban development put increasing pressure on agriculture, CSFS students are working to develop pathways and practices for a sustainable world.

Agriculture on campus has been part of UBC since 1915, when a herd of 24 imported Scottish Ayrshire cattle freely grazed on campus. In the 1970s a new dairy barn was built on the land for the Department of Animal Science—housing facilities for cows, sheep, pigs, birds and aquaculture. Other areas of the south campus fields were used by the departments of plant science, botany and forest sciences.

As these programs closed or moved to new locations, use of the south campus lands declined; by the late 1990s, UBC's new community plan designated them for future housing. But in 1999 students in the faculty now known as Land and Food Systems (formerly called Agricultural Sciences) pushed to re-envision the area as a space for applied research in sustainable agriculture.

So began the fight to save UBC Farm. Beginning in 2008, a new student club, Friends of the UBC Farm, rallied students, graduates, faculty and community groups to have the land preserved as agricultural space in alignment with UBC's sustainability goals. The Friends signed 16,000 people onto their petition and organized a 2,000-strong "Great Farm Trek" march of supporters—from the Student Union Building to the farm—that drew a public statement of support from David Suzuki.

facing In 2010, the AMS worked with the UBC SEEDS Sustainability Program to create a rooftop garden with community garden plots at the Nest. The garden is managed by a student club, Roots on the Roof.

above Thousands of supporters rallied to save UBC Farm, and it is now part of the Centre for Sustainable Food Systems.

UBC administrators eventually agreed to preserve the land. In 2011 the farm was rezoned with the appropriately hybrid title of "green academic" and given a new designation as the Centre for Sustainable Food Systems. Its mission: "Innovation from field to fork to achieve resilient, thriving, and socially just food systems for all."

UBC Farm today is a generator of valuable research on sustainable agriculture and produces 200 varieties of certified organic fruits and vegetables.

Along with its many other offerings to the Vancouver community—drop-in gardening sessions, tours, lectures, pick-your-own berries, cooking classes and a farmers' market—since 2014 the farm has been the site of the wildly popular Farmhouse Fest, a summer craft beer and cider festival.

above With a mission to help "achieve resilient, thriving, and socially just food systems for all," UBC Farm encompasses nearly 60 acres of orchards, fields, pasture and teaching gardens.

FOSTERING SUSTAINABILITY

Conclusion

Leadership for the Future

AS UBC ENTERS its second century, the trends shaping our collective future are disruptive and dynamic. The coming decades will be full of promise, uncertainty and compelling challenges that will require innovation and ethical courage. We need leaders at every level.

Back in 1922, UBC students had the pluck to take the *Tuum Est* (It Is Yours) motto to heart and demand a better university and a better future for themselves. Over the ensuing decades, the UBC community has revised and expanded that time-honoured dictum to mean something along the lines of "The world is yours to improve, restore and protect."

Here's hoping that UBC students keep it up—and that their university continues to provoke and inspire leadership, generosity and deep approaches to sustainability in Canada and around the globe.

facing Students, staff and faculty recreate the famous UBC Great Trek photo at centennial celebrations in 2015.

Timeline

1908

1913

1915

1918

1921

1922

Pre-1908:
For over 4,000 years, the area near the Vancouver campus serves as a Musqueam village site.

1908:
UBC is created, at least on paper, when the BC legislature signs *An Act to Establish and Incorporate a University for the Province of British Columbia.*

1910:
Point Grey is selected as the location of choice for the new university campus.

1913:
Frank F. Wesbrook is appointed as the university's first president.

1915:
Despite World War I having broken out the year before, UBC welcomes 379 students to their first classes in "shacks" in Vancouver's Fairview area. The student society forms this year and calls itself the Alma Mater Society (AMS).

1918:
Student newspaper *The Ubyssey* puts out its first issues, funded by a $2 student fee.

1921:
After a front-page editorial in *The Ubyssey* advocates for a dean of women to advise female students, the university appoints Mary Louise Bollert as UBC's advisor on women. She becomes the first dean of women in 1922 and holds the position for 20 years.

1922:
As part of their "Build the University" campaign, 1,178 UBC students participate in the Great Trek, marching with banners, floats and musical instruments from downtown Vancouver to Point Grey to demand the provincial government finally build the university in its promised location.

1925

1948

1970

1978

1925:
Students attend the first classes
on the Point Grey campus
in several newly completed
buildings.

1940:
Funded with $80,000 in
grants, loans and donations
from students, graduates and
the general public, the AMS
celebrates the opening of the first
student union building. Originally
named Brock Memorial Hall to
honour Dean Reginald Brock and
his wife, Mildred—donors to the
project who had died in a plane
crash in 1935—the name is later
shortened to Brock Hall.

1948:
During halftime of the
homecoming football game,
Kwakwa̲ka'wakw carver Ellen
Neel, her husband Ed, and
Kwikwasut'inuxw Haxwa'mis
Chief William Scow present UBC
and the AMS with the carved
Victory Through Honour pole
topped with a Thunderbird—
and give their community's
permission for UBC to use the
Thunderbird name and symbol in
university athletic programs.

1970:
In partnership with Simon Fraser
University, the University of
Victoria and the University of
Alberta, UBC begins construction
of a cyclotron particle accelerator
as part of the TRIUMF project, a
national laboratory for nuclear
and particle physics research.

1978:
Students kick off the inaugural
Storm the Wall event, which
combines swimming, running,
cycling and scaling a 3.7-metre
wall.

1993:
Chemistry professor Michael
Smith wins the Nobel Prize for his
research on genetic mutations.

2001

2005

2010

1997:
UBC becomes Canada's first university to adopt a sustainable development policy.

2001:
In November UBC opens its downtown Vancouver Robson Square location, which now encompasses 81,000 square feet of classroom and meeting spaces.

2005:
The UBC Okanagan campus opens on the former location of Okanagan University College in Kelowna, with an initial enrolment of 3,500 students. At the opening ceremony, UBC signs a memorandum of understanding on educational cooperation and programming with the Syilx Okanagan Nation, acknowledging the need for strong ties between the university and the Indigenous peoples of the BC Interior.

2006:
UBC signs a memorandum of affiliation with the Musqueam community on whose traditional territory the main Vancouver campus is built. The memorandum notes that UBC "is interested in fostering research, educational and community programs" with the Musqueam community and that both parties "understand the importance of building a long-term relationship."

2010:
UBC joins with the Max Planck Society in a partnership to advance quantum materials research and innovation. In 2017 the University of Tokyo joins the partnership to form the Max Planck–UBC–UTokyo Centre for Quantum Materials.

2010:
UBC Robson Square and the Doug Mitchell Thunderbird Sports Centre are used as host sites for the Vancouver 2010 Olympic and Paralympic Winter Games.

2015:
In September UBC marks the beginning of its 100-year anniversary. On September 30 the university live-broadcasts a centennial launch ceremony that coincides with the grand opening of the newly built Robert H. Lee Alumni Centre. In a nearby square, 1,000 students, faculty, staff and graduates recreate the 1922 Great Trek UBC photo.

2017:
Founded by the Liu Institute for Global Issues and the Institute of Asian Research, the School of Public Policy and Global Affairs launches as an interdisciplinary hub for exploring local and global issues—and seeking policy solutions that will change the world for the better.

2017

2018

2017:
The 17-metre *Reconciliation Pole* is mounted on Main Mall. Carved from an 800-year-old cedar by Haida carver James Hart (7idansuu), the pole tells the story of the impact of residential schools on Indigenous peoples in Canada.

2017:
Made possible by a grant from Microsoft, the University of Washington and UBC announce the creation of the Cascadia Urban Analytics Cooperative, which will use research and data to help cities address ongoing issues such as traffic and homelessness.

2018:
UBC launches the School of Biomedical Engineering, a partnership between the Faculty of Medicine and the Faculty of Applied Science. In a joint statement, the deans of both faculties promise that the new school will "break down antiquated academic boundaries" and work on "applying an engineering mindset to disease prevention, diagnosis and treatment."

2018:
The newly built Indian Residential School History and Dialogue Centre opens in April. An "institution of memory" focused on the tragic history of residential schools, it offers space for survivors (and their families and communities) to learn and talk about their experiences—and a place for developing educational materials to ensure this chapter of Canadian history is not forgotten.

Acknowledgements

THE AUTHOR WOULD like to extend his thanks to all those who helped bring this book together, including UBC president Santa Ono for his many contributions; Terry Lavender for help with vision, text and editing; Matt Warburton and Frances Verzosa for help in getting the project underway; Alicia Margono for assistance in research, photo sourcing and copy editing; Paul Joseph and other photographic contributors for their excellent work; Kevin Ward for his assistance with Indigenous material; Chief Wayne Sparrow and Larry Grant of the Musqueam community for graciously allowing the use of their words; Herbert Rosengarten for help catalyzing the project and reviewing the manuscript; Janis Letchumanan and Chris Pollon for their help in research and writing; Richard Fisher for his assistance in looking over the manuscript; and the many UBC department heads and communications experts who helped correct and edit these entries.

Last but certainly not least, my gratitude to the fine people at Figure 1 Publishing for helping conceptualize, design, edit and print this very attractive book, including Chris Labonté, Lara Smith, Jessica Sullivan, Lana Okerlund and Renate Preuss.

Selected Sources

Books

Damer, Eric, and Herbert Rosengarten. *UBC: The First 100 Years*. Vancouver: University of British Columbia, 2009.

Goldfarb, Sheldon. *The Hundred-Year Trek: A History of UBC's Alma Mater Society*. Victoria: Heritage House, 2017.

Stewart, Lee. *It's Up to You: Women at UBC in the Early Years*. Vancouver: University of British Columbia Press, 1990.

Online Sources

University of British Columbia

100.ubc.ca
aboriginal.ubc.ca
academic.ubc.ca
acam.arts.ubc.ca
allard.ubc.ca
alumnicentre.ubc.ca
ams.ubc.ca
anth.ubc.ca

archives.library.ubc.ca
arts.ubc.ca
asia.ubc.ca
brand.ubc.ca
beatymuseum.ubc.ca
belkin.ubc.ca
botanicalgarden.ubc.ca
calendar.ubc.ca
campusplanning.ok.ubc.ca
centennial.aboriginal.ubc.ca
chung.library.ubc.ca
cirs.ubc.ca
collections.library.ubc.ca
cs.ubc.ca
ctlt.ubc.ca
cwsei.ubc.ca
democracy.arts.ubc.ca
dvc.ok.ubc.ca
educ.ubc.ca
entrepreneurship.ubc.ca
events.ubc.ca
faculty.canvas.ubc.ca
facultystaff.students.ubc.ca
faculty-staff.ubc.ca

fhis.ubc.ca
fnel.arts.ubc.ca
forestry.ubc.ca
grad.ubc.ca
historyproject.allard.ubc.ca
icics.ubc.ca
ikblc.ubc.ca
infrastructuredevelopment.ubc.ca
ires.ubc.ca
japanese-canadian-student-tribute.ubc.ca
journalism.ubc.ca
koerner.library.ubc.ca
learningexchange.ubc.ca
library.ubc.ca
math.ubc.ca
med.ubc.ca
mmru.ubc.ca
moa.ubc.ca
music.ubc.ca
nanomat.chem.ubc.ca
news.ok.ubc.ca
oceans.ubc.ca
ok.ubc.ca

open.library.ubc.ca

phas.ubc.ca

president.ubc.ca

pwias.ubc.ca

qmi.ubc.ca

rbsarchives.library.ubc.ca

recreation.ubc.ca

research.ubc.ca

robsonsquare.ubc.ca

sauder.ubc.ca

sba.ubc.ca

scarp.ubc.ca

science.ubc.ca

sportfacilities.ubc.ca

spph.ubc.ca

star.ubc.ca

strategicplan.ubc.ca

students.ok.ubc.ca

students.ubc.ca

support.ubc.ca

sustain.ubc.ca

theatrefilm.ubc.ca

thrive.ubc.ca

trekmagazine.alumni.ubc.ca

ubcfarm.ubc.ca

vancouver.housing.ubc.ca

you.ubc.ca

zoology.ubc.ca

221A, 221a.ca

Abel Prize, abelprize.no

Academica Group, academica.ca

Academy of Motion Picture Arts
and Sciences, oscars.org

All Native Basketball Tournament,
anbt.ca

Architect magazine,
architectmagazine.com

B+H Architects, bharchitects.com

Bamfield Marine Sciences Centre,
bamfieldmsc.com

BC Hydro, bchydro.com

BC Sports Hall of Fame,
bcsportshalloffame.com

Bird, bird.ca

British Columbia Centre for
Excellence in HIV/AIDS,
cfenet.ubc.ca

Canadian Architect,
canadianarchitect.com

Canadian Encyclopedia,
thecanadianencyclopedia.ca

Canadian Medical Hall of Fame,
cdnmedhall.org

Canadian Olympic Team, olympic.ca

Canadian Theatre Encyclopedia,
canadiantheatre.com

Car Talk, cartalk.com

Cascadia Urban Analytics
Cooperative, cascadiadata.org

CBC Music, cbcmusic.ca

CBC News, cbc.ca

Centaur Products,
centaurproducts.com

Centre for Digital Media, thecdm.ca

Centre for Molecular Medicine and
Therapeutics, cmmt.ubc.ca

Chan Centre for the Performing Arts,
chancentre.com

Cinephile, cinephile.ca

City of Vancouver Archives,
searcharchives.vancouver.ca

ConstructConnect, canada.
constructconnect.com

Cyberpunk Project, project.
cyberpunk.ru

Daily Hive, dailyhive.com

Desi Today, desitoday.ca

Discover Wesbrook,
discoverwesbrook.com

Douglas Reynolds Gallery,
douglasreynoldsgallery.com

Dr. Peter AIDS Foundation,
drpeter.org

Encyclopedia Brittanica,
britannica.com

Gitxaala Nation, gitxaalanation.com

Global Impact Investing Network,
thegiin.org

Global News, globalnews.ca

Globe and Mail,
theglobeandmail.com

Go Thunderbirds, gothunderbirds.ca

HCMA Architecture and Design, hcma.ca

History of Canadian Broadcasting, broadcasting-history.ca

Indigitization, indigitization.ca

Inside Higher Ed, insidehighered.com

International Scholarships Program, scholarships-bourses.gc.ca

Johns Hopkins Center for American Indian Health, caih.jhu.edu

John Simon Guggenheim Memorial Foundation, gf.org

Justice Institute of British Columbia, jibc.ca

Kelowna Capital News, kelownacapnews.com

Kelowna Now, kelownanow.com

KPMB Architects, kpmb.com

Kwantlen Polytechnic University, kpu.ca

Library and Archives Canada, bac-lac.gc.ca

LiveScience, livescience.com

Maclean's, macleans.ca

Matthew Alun Brown, matthewalunbrown.com

Media Group Tajikistan, news.tj

MemoryBC, memorybc.ca

Mendeley, mendeley.com

Metro Vancouver, metrovancouver.org

Michael Smith Foundation for Health Research, msfhr.org

Musqueam, musqueam.bc.ca

Nebula Awards, nebulas.sfwa.org

Networks of Centres of Excellence, nce-rce.gc.ca

Nobel Prize, nobelprize.org

Now Toronto, nowtoronto.com

Order of British Columbia, orderofbc.gov.bc.ca

Physics Today, physicstoday.scitation.org

Pollinator Partnership, pollinator.org

Prince George Citizen, princegeorgecitizen.com

Project Seahorse, projectseahorse.org

Province of British Columbia News Archive, archive.news.gov.bc.ca

Quanta Magazine, quantamagazine.org

Reciprocal Research Network, rrncommunity.org

Research2Reality, research2reality.com

Rowing Canada, rowingcanada.org

Science.ca, science.ca

Science Fiction Awards and Database, sfadb.com

Simon Fraser University, journals.sfu.ca

Sports Reference, sports-reference.com

Thirty Meter Telescope, tmt.org

Toronto Star, thestar.com

TRIUMF, triumf.ca

Ubyssey, ubyssey.ca

University of Central Asia, ucentralasia.org

University of Oxford Department of Physics, www2.physics.ox.ac.uk

University of the Fraser Valley, ufv.ca

Vancouver Sun, vancouversun.com

Vancouver Symphony Orchestra, vancouversymphony.ca

Vancouver Writers Festival, writersfest.bc.ca

Virtual Museum of Asian Canadian Cultural Heritage, vmacch.ca

VSO Orchestral Institute, vsoinstitute.ca

William Gibson, williamgibsonbooks.com

Wize Monkey, wizemonkey.com

Photo Credits

AMS Archives, 101, 102, 107

Boeing, 122

Lara Therrien Boulos, 55 (left)

Grant Callegari/Hakai Institute, 169

Centre for Digital Media, 44 (top), 45

Dr. Peter AIDS Foundation, 121

Edward Chang, 59, 61

Chinese Student Association, 74 (bottom right)

CHIME, 111

CiTR, 104

Data Science Institute, 115

Martin Dee / UBC Brand & Marketing, i, 6, 8, 14, 17, 22, 42, 43, 68–69, 75, 95, 126 (bottom), 136–37, 145, 162–63, 178, 179 (top and bottom right), 180, 185 (2017)

Michael Elkan, 81

Don Erhardt / UBC Brand & Marketing, vi, 19 (left), 29 (left), 32, 88, 108–109, 113, 116, 118, 120, 152, 153, 154, 165, 167

Faculty of Medicine, 33

GISAU, 74 (top right)

Timothy Hogan, 97 (top left)

Eric Johnson, 55 (right)

Francis Jones, 46

Paul H. Joseph / UBC Brand & Marketing, 7, 12, 19 (top), 29 (centre and right), 52, 63, 65, 70, 71, 72, 78, 91, 96, 97 (bottom left, centre and right), 117, 126 (top), 143, 147 (left), 148, 155, 170, 171, 185 (2015), 185 (2018)

Paul H. Joseph / UBC Okanagan, 2, 15, 16

Clare Kiernan / UBC, 37

Rich Lam, 146

Justin Lee / UBC, 149

Nic Lehoux, 86

Jenny Lu, 67

Alicia Margono / UBC, 21, 77, 82, 83, 85, 92, 93 (bottom), 98, 105, 106, 147 (right), 175 (bottom)

Kareem M. Negm, 44 (bottom)

Santa J. Ono, 161

Emma Peter, 87

PRINT Arts and Crafts Club, 103

Psychology Student Association, 74 (bottom left)

Sarah Race, 174

Jamil Rhajiak / UBC, 142, 179 (left)

Peter SPURRIER / Alamy Stock Photo, 140 (bottom)

TRIUMF, 133, 134, 135

UBC, 47, 57, 94, 97 (top right), 138, 139

UBC Athletics & Recreation, 144

UBC Botanical Garden, 172

UBC Brand & Marketing, 93 (top), 173, 175 (top)

UBC Centennial, 182 (1908), 182 (1913), 182 (1918), 183 (1925), 184 (2010)

UBC Centre for the Study of Democratic Institutions, 128, 129

UBC Department of Asian Studies, 35, 36

UBC Department of Computer Science, 123

UBC Ethnographic Film Unit, 51

UBC Faculty of Medicine, 34

UBC Go Global, 66

UBC / Hover Collective, ii–iii, iv, 3–5, 30–31, 79, 124, 150–51, 156, 176

UBC Institute for Computing, Information and Cognitive Systems, 131, 132

UBC Library Archives, 50, 157, 158

UBC Okanagan, 18, 24 (top), 76, 89

The Ubyssey, 99

University of British Columbia Archives, 9 [1.1/16570], 10, 11, 13, 24 (bottom) [35.1/228-3], 25 (top) [1.1/13019], 25 (bottom) [35.1/635], 54, 84, 182 (1915), 182 (1921), 182 (1922), 183 (1948), 183 (1970), 183 (1978), 184 (2001) [44.1/3229-1], 184 (2005) [44.1/1912]

UTSAV, 73, 74 (top left)

Amanda Vincent, 168

Wilson Wong, UBC Athletics and Recreation, 140 (top)

Index

Photos are in *italic* unless on another indexed page. The terms *faculty, department* and *school* were omitted for brevity.

191

Cataloguing data are available from Library
and Archives Canada

ISBN 978-1-77327-088-3 (hbk.)

Design by Jessica Sullivan
Editing and indexing by Lana Okerlund
Proofreading by Renate Preuss

Front jacket and cover photograph by
UBC Brand & Marketing / Hover Collective
Back jacket photograph by Don Erhardt /
UBC Brand & Marketing

Printed and bound in Canada by Friesens
Distributed internationally by Publishers Group West

Figure 1 Publishing Inc.
Vancouver BC Canada
www.figure1publishing.com